The
World
as a
Total
System

KENNETH E. BOULDING

The World as a Total System

 SAGE PUBLICATIONS Beverly Hills London New Delhi

For information address:

SAGE Publications, Inc.
275 South Beverly Drive
Beverly Hills, California 90212

SAGE Publications India Pvt. Ltd.
M-32 Market
Greater Kailash I
New Delhi 110 048 India

SAGE Publications Ltd
28 Banner Street
London EC1Y 8QE
England

Printed in the United States of America

Library of Congress Cataloging in Publication Data

Boulding, Kenneth Ewart, 1910-
  The world as a total system.

  "This volume is based on a series of lectures
presented at the United Nations University, Tokyo,
Japan, January/February 1984."
  "September 1984."
  Includes index.
  1. Civilization—Addresses, essays, lectures.
2. Social systems—Addresses, essays, lectures.
3. System theory—Addresses, essays, lectures.
I. Title.
HM201.B68 1985   909   85-1823
ISBN 0-8039-2443-7

FIRST PRINTING

CONTENTS

INTRODUCTION

The roots of this volume go back a long way in my own thinking—certainly to my interest in general systems, which developed in the late 1940s and early 1950s—and resulted in my being a founding father, in 1954, of what is now the Society for General Systems Research. My year in Japan at the International Christian University in 1963-1964 led me to a renewed interest in evolutionary theory, which produced *A Primer on Social Dynamics* in 1970 and *Ecodynamics* in 1978. This volume in a sense represents the convergence of these two streams: looking at the earth as a general system in the evolutionary pattern but also, of course, as a complex structure of many different systems. The immediate occasion of these two streams coming together was a series of seminars which I gave at the United Nations University in Tokyo in January and February 1984 on the theme that is the title of this volume. I expanded these five seminars, which were written only in outline form, into the present volume during April 1984 when I was a visiting professor at Mesa College in Grand Junction, Colorado, teaching a course in the subject of this volume.

My intellectual debts are too numerous and too large even to be acknowledged. I am particularly grateful, however, to Rector Soedjatmoko, the professional staff, and the many friends I made at the United Nations University and the stimulating discussions and conversations I had there. I am grateful, too, to Mesa College for a most delightful month with enough stimulation from colleagues and students to keep me actively thinking, and enough leisure to get the book dictated. Again, I must thank Mrs. Vivian Wilson, my administrative assistant of seventeen years' standing at the University of Colorado in Boulder, without whose editing, advice, and organizing capacity this volume would never have emerged into print. My thanks, also, to Ms. Susan Dunahay for skillfully transcribing and producing this volume on the word processor.

It is particularly appropriate that the United Nations University should have played a significant role in the formation of this volume, for indeed learning about the world as a total system is precisely what the United Nations University is all about and what makes it so distinctive. The United Nations University is a symbol of the fact that the world is a total system as well as a mosaic of partial systems. It is much more than a set of quarrelsome national systems, although these too are part of the whole and to be respected as such. It is my hope that this volume, as small and inadequate as it is, may help to provoke a movement among the educational systems of the world for both research and teaching about the world as a total system, so that we may all come to see ourselves and our own cultures and countries as rightly close and important to us, but also as finding their greatest significance as parts of a larger whole.

—*Kenneth E. Boulding*

CHAPTER 1

What Systems Can We Perceive in the World?

The broadest possible definition of a system is that it is "anything that is not chaos." We could turn the definition around and define a system as any structure that exhibits order and pattern. The orderly structures and patterns of which we are most immediately aware are those within our own minds, bodies, and behavior, but virtually all human beings have a strong conviction that corresponding to these patterns of mind and body are similar patterns in what might be called the "real world." We are also convinced that there are some pattern structures that we know and some, probably a great many, that we do not know. We have an enormous storehouse of images and structures within our minds to which we have access through consciousness and memory. These are undoubtedly coded in the structure of the brain and the nervous system, although exactly how this is done is still not really known. The brain also stores a great many structures to which we do not have immediate access—things we have forgotten, names we cannot remember, and the vast underworld of the Freudian unconscious. When we recollect that we have as many neurons in the brain as there are stars in a galaxy, it is not surprising that the brain is able to code orderly structures of great complexity. Some of these we recognize as fantasy—characters in a novel, gods of Olympus, dungeons and dragons—which we recognize as having no exact counterpart in the real world. Other images, like our image of the house where we live, of our friends and relations, our neighborhood, the map of the world, our ability to play tennis, we regard as "true"—that is, corresponding with structures in the real world into which they "map" (as a mathematician would say), although the mapping will not necessarily be complete or perfect.

The systems with which we are most concerned, therefore, are those created by the human learning process in our minds that are true. Learning is a process very similar to evolution (Pringle, 1956). The human brain is a remarkably active structure, constantly producing patterns within it that are capable of being perceived in consciousness as images. We see this even in dreams. Indeed, the main product of the human brain might be described as structures that turn into fantasies or images within the mind. This process is much like mutation in evolution.

Then there is a large process of selection of these images by a great variety of processes of testing by which some images are selected as true and others as not true. We do this constantly in daily life in what can be called "folk knowledge." We have an image of our friend's house derived from some previous experience, we go there and find that it is all shut up or has burned down, and our previous image is rejected as untrue and a new image is substituted for it. Testing almost always involves some expectations or prediction that either is or is not fulfilled as time moves into the future. Preceding this empirical testing, however, there is always a complex process of logical testing and deduction within the human mind that permits us to create an expectation. Even in such a simple matter as going to a friend's house, our image of its location is determined by a complex set of experiences and deductions. We must know about means of transportation and directions, the significance of addresses, and we must have confidence in these. We must deduce from past experience that our friend is indeed our friend. Even such a simple act as visiting a friend's house turns out to be a very complex process.

What might be called "scholarly knowledge," which would include both the humanities and the sciences, differs from folk knowledge only in its extent, complexity, and criteria of what is evidence. Scholarly knowledge also might be described as testable fantasy. This consists of images of Henry VIII, of Buddha, of chemical formulae, of quarks, of DNA, or of an equilibrium of relative prices. These are constantly subject to mutation, new ideas, new structures that are by no means random and that often come out of a perception of a problem and an attempt to solve it. Then there is a constant process of testing by comparison of records, manuscripts, archaeological remains, recorded positions of the planets, records of previous experiments, observations in the field, and so on. These complex processes of testing reinforce our belief in the truth of some images and destroy our belief in the truth of others. Like the overall processes of evolution, this process of human learning has a certain "time's arrow," simply because the testing process makes error—that is, images that are not true—a little less stable than those that are true or have greater degrees of truth. One problem is that untestable images often may be more stable than testable ones, even when they are in error. The fact that we are surrounded by a real world, however, introduces a bias toward truth into the learning process, no matter how much we wall ourselves against it.

One thing of which we become aware very early in the human learning process is that structures have parts, and that an important aspect of the systematic structure of things is that the relationship among its parts is an important element in the structure and behavior of any system. Quite early we become aware of our body as a structure, that it has hands, fingers, nails, eyes, ears, and so on. Internal rumblings and heartbeats give us a clue even to its internal structure. We become aware that our family has different members— father, mother, brothers, and sisters; that our house has windows, doors, and a roof; that a car has wheels, an engine, and so on.

Scholarly knowledge carries this process much further. Our neighborhood is part of the globe of the Earth. We see the Earth as part of the solar system that is part of a galaxy that is part of a universe. Furthermore, we see that our body consists not only of organs in great variety but of cells, of atoms and electrons, of energy structures, and so on. There is a hierarchy of size of systems, from the quark or the photon to the total universe. Each level of the hierarchy interacts with levels both above it and below it. DNA may help to plan the organism, but the interaction of organisms determines what genetic structures will survive. A virus may give us a fever through its impact on both the chemistry of the body and its organs. Hypnosis can change our bodily chemistry. There was a moment of reductionism in the history of science when it was believed that each level of the hierarchy was determined by the levels below it. This view is very hard to sustain today.

An important question—especially for this volume, where we are trying to look at the Earth as a total system—is that of the degree of isolation of systems and structures. We certainly can form some kind of image in our minds of the total system of the Earth at any one time, in a descriptive way. The extent to which the Earth is a total system of interacting parts, however, and the degree to which it is a pattern of isolated systems that have little or no impact on each other is an important question to which I shall return constantly. There may well be other planets in the universe that are capable of developing advanced forms of life. If there are, as far as we know they have not interacted with us and represent isolated systems. Even isolated systems can, however, exhibit similar patterns of development. We see this even on the Earth. America developed agriculture, cities, and empires with structures in many ways similar in structure to those of the old world but, as far as we know, without any contact between them. The similarities developed because human learning processes have a rather similar structure for all human beings. We are pretty sure that chimpanzees would never build pyramids, no matter where they were.

Let us now proceed to a description of the major kinds of systematic structures we perceive in our minds that we believe are characteristic of the real world. Here we are looking at something like a hierarchy of complexity rather than of size, although it is also true that larger structures have a greater potential for complexity than smaller ones. The first and most basic pattern in this hierarchy could be described as *static* or *descriptive structures*–flashlight photographs, as it were, of structures at a moment in time. The most fundamental category here consists of structures in space. These are represented by maps, diagrams, chemical formulae, DNA, star charts, anatomy, architectural plans, and drawings. The representations of these structures, both in our minds and in human artifacts, like maps, pictures, and drawings, always tend to be a good deal simpler than the structures as they exist in the real world.

These simplified images are made by abstraction—that is, by selecting out those elements in the real-world structure that are most important to us. A map is a good example. A road map shows the roads but usually not every individual house or individual tree. No map ever shows each individual blade of grass, or even individual human beings. Maps, or even three-dimensional models of human anatomy, never show individual blood cells. Sometimes we express structures exhibiting analogies to spatial relations by charts, such as organization charts or flowcharts with arrows connecting various parts. These can easily be misleading, although they can also be useful.

Another method of describing static structures is by lists, in which we enumerate and identify the parts of a system. A card catalogue in a library is a good example. It is a kind of alphabetical map in what is called a "lexicographic ordering," which, together with a map of the library, enables us to find a book. The invention of the alphabet was a great step forward here, in that it enabled any word to be placed in a position of what is essentially a list of real numbers.

Even lists with an arbitrary order can be quite instructive, like the balance sheets of firms or items in a budget. Statistical descriptions are another form of list. Thus with a given population we can list an age distribution—how many members of the population are between zero and one year old, between one and two years old, and so on—or an income distribution—how many people in the country have incomes between $0 and $1000, between $1000 and $2000, and so on.

The next step involves the description of dynamic systems—that is, of changes in static structures over time. These really consist of four-dimensional structures (three dimensions of space and one of time), but as our minds cannot readily visualize such structures, we often have to reduce them to one or two dimensions of space and one of time. A good example would be the reel of a movie. Each frame is a static structure. The whole reel represents changes in the structure over time. When it is shown on a movie projector, we actually perceive it on the screen as continuous change over time of a two-dimensional structure or, if it is a stereo movie, of a three-dimensional structure. It is interesting that a three-dimensional structure can be perceived by projecting two slightly different two-dimensional pictures onto the screen.

Three-dimensional figures with two dimensions of space and one of time, which might be called time cubes, are valuable in visualizing the description of dynamic systems. Thus suppose we have a map of the world as of today on transparent paper. If we put a similar map for yesterday immediately below the first, then one for two days ago, three days ago, and so on, as far back as we wish, we end up with something like a transparent cube, with time going vertically and the changes in the map as solid shapes in the cube. Thus we could visualize the life of a person in such a time cube as a dot on each of the transparent maps. The person then appears as a long thread originating at conception, traveling around the world, and ending in death. We could then go one step further and visualize the cube as containing the 80 or so billion human beings who have ever lived, originating perhaps in Africa and spreading all around the rest of the world, like a great mass of spaghetti, each thread originating where two other threads, the father and the mother, cross.

The role of numbers in the description of both static and dynamic systems is significant. Thus the position in space relative to some arbitrary point of origin of every point on the Earth's surface can be described by three numbers: latitude, longitude, and altitude. A list of these numbers might be described as a nonintelligible description of the spatial structure of the Earth's surface. If it is to become intelligible, the numbers must be translated into maps, which can, however, be done fairly easily. This can even be done by a computer. The numbers contain the same structure of information as the map, but if we had a list of them it would not convey very much to us. In a sense, the numbers are also arbitrary, depending on the zero points on the units of measurement, and are merely an arbitrary type of description of a real world that consists not of numbers as such but of shapes, sizes, structures, patterns, and positions.

Nevertheless, because in many ways the human mind can manipulate numbers more easily than it can manipulate structures, numbers are very useful as a mental tool, particularly in regard to systems of more than three dimensions. We see this use, for instance, in the description of the solar system in terms of the succession of positions of the planets and other bodies that make up the solar system. Observation of the position of a planet in the sphere of the sky, again, can be represented by three numbers: its latitude (declination) and longitude (right ascension) in the sky and its distance from the Earth. The distance from the Earth is calculated by parallax—that is, measuring its position in the sky simultaneously from two different places on the Earth's surface. This gives us a three-dimensional structure, much as we have in a stereo film. We can then simplify the dynamic pattern enormously by reducing it to a set of equations, as Laplace finally did. These can be expressed either as difference equations, which express a stable relationship between the position of the system today and its position tomorrow, or differential equations, which express stable rates of change of diverse variables.

Here we are really edging toward the next great category of systems, which is *explanatory systems*. These do not merely describe a pattern of structures in space and time, but try to explain this pattern in terms of some basic regularities that are, in some sense, necessary. David Hume distinguished between constant connection, which is an observed description of some relationship in the system, and necessary connection, which is what we tend to mean by cause and effect. The study of constant connection is correlation, the observation and description of things that go together. Correlation, however, is not causation. It can happen by accident or because two things are following the same inner dynamic pattern. For twins separated and raised in different households, the age of one will be remarkably well correlated with the height of the other for a considerable period, although there is no connection between the two.

Observation, especially a casual observation of empirical regularities, easily leads into superstition—that is, the perception of an order that is not really there—and this perception often has a distressing tendency to justify itself because the cases that will reinforce it tend to be observed and noted selectively over the cases that do not reinforce it. This is particularly likely to happen where the expectations that result from the belief are vague. Astrology is a good example. The predictions of astrologers are usually vague enough so that almost anything that happens confirms them. I myself have had some remarkably accurate predictions from Chinese fortune cookies, but I attribute these to good luck on the part of the cookie makers rather than to esoteric knowledge.

The perception of systems usually begins with the perception of identities—that is, relationships that cannot be otherwise from the very definition of the things related. This is why mathematics is useful in the development of systems. Mathematics, on the whole, is the perception of identities, although it sometimes takes a lot of analysis to perceive them, and we have to be careful because identities that are perceived in one context, as in Euclidean geometry, do not always apply in another context. A good example is what might be called the *demographic identity,* which I have sometimes called the "bathtub theorem," the bathtub being a good example of it. This is the principle that the increase in anything is equal to the additions minus the subtractions. Additions are equal to "births"—that is, new items produced—plus inmigrations from outside the system; subtractions are equal to "deaths"—that is, the consumption or disappearance of items—plus outmigrations. This principle applies to water in the bathtub: If more is coming in than is going out, the amount of water will increase. It also applies to all populations, whether of atoms, molecules, organisms, human beings, or human artifacts.

Somewhat related is the conservation theorem: that anything that has a fixed quantity can only be redistributed among the parts of a system; an increase in one place must be offset by a decrease in other places. This applies to energy or matter or "mattergy." It applies to human time—we have only 24 hours in a day, and if we devote more to one thing we have to devote less to others. If there is a fixed quantity of money in a system, then the sum of all balances of payments is zero—that is, money simply is a shifting cargo, shifting around among the owners. An increase in money stock in one place necessitates a decrease elsewhere. Gertrude Stein once put it succinctly: "Money never changes, it is only the pockets that change." If there is an increase in the quantity—that is, the total stock—of money, the sum of all balances of payments in a closed system would be equal to that increase.

In addition to the identities there are propositions about the real world that might be called "near-identities," which *almost* have to be true. A good example is something that might be called the "Generalized Second Law," of which the Second Law of Thermodynamics is a special case. This is the principle that if anything happens there must have been a potential for its happening, and that after it has happened that potential has been used up. The Second Law of Thermodynamics expresses this in terms of entropy, which is really negative thermodynamic potential, a rather awkward concept. Thus an increase in entropy is the same thing as a diminution in thermodynamic potential. Something like the Generalized Second Law is found in a great many different systems. When something falls or flows downhill, it had more gravitational potential at the top of the hill than it had at the bottom. A fertilized egg contains biological potential for creating the appropriate organism. In the process of creating it, the potential is gradually used up until finally it is all used up and the organism dies. Any act of production, whether of a chicken from an egg or a house from a blueprint, involves a potential that is used up in the course of the production process. These "entropic" processes of the using up of potential are almost universal in all systems.

On the other hand, they may be offset by the recreation of potential through anti-entropic processes. Water exhausts its gravitational potential as it flows downstream, but then it rains upstream because the earth is an open system of constant throughput of energy from the sun. Soil erodes and is then replaced by the decomposition of rock and the activity of the soil organisms. Biological potential is exhausted by aging, but every time a new egg is fertilized it is re-created. Organizations rigidify and decay, and the occupants of their essential roles then retire or die and are replaced by younger people who may rejuvenate the organization.

Many of these near-identities relate to human behavior. Economists, for instance, are firmly convinced that when making a choice, everybody does what he or she thinks is best at the time. This is called the "theory of maximizing behavior," and it seems hard to deny. What determines the agendas of choice and what determines the valuations that people put on various alternatives is another matter, and much more complex and less obvious.

Logic and identities, of course, are not enough. We constantly run into systems that could have been other than what they are. These require empirical study, observation, and records. The more careful the observation and the records, the more likely we are to discover structures in the empirical world that are stable and exhibit persistent patterns through time. Thus the conservation principle is an identity, but the question as to what is actually conserved—that is, what there is a fixed quantity of—can only be answered empirically. It used to be matter and energy separately. Now that we have discovered that each can be transformed into the other, it has to be matter and energy together, sometimes called "mattergy." The question as to whether there is a fixed quantity of money in a given period is something that can only be answered empirically, and so on.

The methodology of empirical investigation should depend heavily on the nature of the system that is being investigated, and a lot of wasted effort—especially in the biological and social sciences—has been caused by attempts to apply a methodology that is quite appropriate, for instance, in celestial mechanics (a system where the basic parameters do not change) to systems that are highly stochastic, probabilistic, and where parameters do change. Again, experimental methods are appropriate in the study of systems that have fairly stable parameters and that are not subject to the occurrence of improbable events, and where the smaller systems that can be studied experimentally have some sort of correspondence with the larger systems we really want to find out about. Experiment is a useful distortion of the real world in a great many cases, and in the physical sciences it has been very fruitful; in the biological and social sciences, much less so. Each of the disciplines has different mixtures of what is appropriate for experiment and what is appropriate for observation.

With this background we can now construct a list—indeed, something of a hierarchy—of systems that we have good reason to believe correspond to something in the real world.

Mechanical Systems

The first of these is mechanical systems, which involve changes of the state of a system that is guided by constant and relatively simple parameters. We have already seen that dynamic systems can be described by difference and differential equations if the parameters are constant and not too complex. In celestial mechanics, for instance, these equations rarely go beyond the third degree—that is, a system that would have constant rates of change of rates of change. A system of the first degree would involve constant rates of change. An object moving at a constant velocity is a good example. Systems of the second degree, like gravitational systems, on the whole operate with a constant rate of change of velocity—that is, constant acceleration. A heavy body falling to the ground is a good example. This example illustrates, incidentally, how careful we have to be about pure empiricism. If gravity had simply been studied by the empirical observation of falling bodies, such as stones, leaves, and feathers, Newton probably would never have discovered the law of gravity because he would not have been able to identify the complexities of the system, such as air resistance. Furthermore, the inverse square law, on which a good deal of Newtonian mechanics is based, is very close to being an identity and rests on the fact that the surface of a sphere is proportional to the square of its radius. Hence if we have some process that radiates out from a point, it will be distributed over an area proportional to the square of the distance from the point, and its intensity therefore will be proportional to 1.0 divided by the square of the distance.

In electricity, Ohm's Law—that current is proportional to the potential difference between two points divided by the resistance—is also a near-identity, for we have to define resistance to conform to it. This principle applies in some degree to any flow system. These mechanical identities are found in living organisms, in such things as the flow of blood through a body or air in the lungs, muscular movements, which depend a good deal on principles of the lever, and so on.

Cybernetic Systems

At a level of complexity a little above that of simple mechanical systems we have cybernetic systems, so called by Norbert Wiener (1948).[1] Examples would be thermostats; a governor in an engine or a phonograph turntable that maintains a constant velocity; and a large number of systems in living bodies—for instance, those that maintain constant blood temperature and pressure, that regulate the chemical composition of many parts of the body, and so on. In living bodies these processes are summed up under the name *homeostasis,* which is Greek for equilibrium. Cybernetic systems differ from simple mechanical equilibria, like that of a pendulum, in that they involve information. They involve three essential elements: a *receptor,* which can detect when the system is not at equilibrium, especially whether it is above or below the variable that is to be be stabilized; a *transmitter,* which then transmits this information to an *effector,* which then has the power of changing the variable.

In a simple thermostat the receptor is a thermometer. If this shows a temperature above what the thermostat is set at (the ideal), the transmitter will relay this information to the furnace and shut it off, so that the system will cool down. If the temperature is below the ideal, the transmitter will relay this information to turn on the furnace, which will warm the system up. This process is called "negative feedback," as the transmitter and the effector operate to reverse processes away from equilibrium in either direction.

There are many such processes in social systems. All organizations, for instance, exhibit some kind of homeostasis of their position statement—that is, the list of quantities significant for the evaluation of different parts of the organizational structure. A considerable amount of business behavior can be accounted for by homeostasis of the balance sheet. Thus when a business sells its final product, inventory diminishes and cash increases. Then the business spends the cash to buy labor, raw materials, and so on in order to restore the inventory of the final product. When the president of the United States finds that his popularity, according to the polls, is diminishing, he is then likely to do things to try to bring his popularity up again. Lovers' quarrels are made up, misunderstandings are cleared up, even wars end in peace, and so on.

Positive Feedback Systems

There are also systems in which the feedback is positive, which would be the case, for instance, if the thermostat turned the furnace on when it got too hot and turned it off when it got too cold. These systems are not uncommon, but they do not usually last for very long. Disequilibrium systems tend to move toward some kind of "system break" at which they change into a different type of system. A good example is a forest fire. The faster it burns, the hotter it gets; the hotter it gets, the faster it burns, until it burns itself out. Even here, however, there are long-run equilibrium cybernetic systems at work. The forest usually eventually restores itself through a succession of ecosystems as long as the seeds are not destroyed or can come into the system from the unburned outside.

In social systems we have things like arms races, where an increase in the arms of country **A** produces an increase in **B**, which produces a further increase in **A**, a further increase in **B**, and so on, rather like a forest fire. This, again, sometimes proceeds to war and a breakdown of the system. Escalating quarrels in individual relationships are rather similar. So, at the other end, is falling in love. **A** does something which makes **B** take an interest in **A**, **A** perceives this and becomes attracted to **B**, **B** perceives this and becomes more fond of **A**, and so on. The whole evolutionary process can be thought of as a gigantic positive feedback: The more complex mutations find niches that create niches for still more complex mutations. We see a similar process in human learning, again, a bit like a forest fire. The more we learn, the easier it is to learn more, especially as we learn about learning. This produces anti-entropic processes that offset the entropic processes of potential exhaustion and decay.

Creodic Systems

Beyond simple equilibrium cybernetic systems we have what biologist Waddington (1962: 64) called "creodes" (from two Greek words meaning "necessary path"), of which the growth of a chicken from an egg (called "morphogenesis") is a good example. The "know-how" contained in the genetic structure organizes this very complex process of growth that has a certain equilibrium time pattern to it. This growth may be hampered by a temporary lack of energy or materials or by disease, poor nutrition, and so on; but if the interruption is not too great, the growth pattern will be resumed. Something rather similar takes place in the growth of a building from an architect's plan, or an organization from the ideas in the mind of a founder. The economic growth of a society, for instance, which is fundamentally a human learning process, may be interrupted for a while by war, like the Civil War in the United States, but the process is usually resumed after the war is over and may even catch up, so that the society gets to the point where it would have been had there been no war, although this does not always happen. The process of a student getting a degree may be interrupted by illness or financial difficulties and may be resumed again roughly where it left off. These processes can be called "planned" in the sense that they are guided by some kind of initial plan, although the plan itself, of course, may be modified as the process proceeds.

Reproductive Systems

All living systems have genetic structures that are not only capable of organizing the growth of the organism but also have the remarkable capacity of reproducing themselves. This is because the genetic instructions are coded in the very complex DNA molecule; the famous double helix, which has the capacity of attracting to itself identical radicals of the amino acids that constitute the code of information and splitting this structure off as a mirror image, which then reproduces the original molecule. A rather primitive form of reproduction is chemical catalysis, in which a certain molecular structure—the catalyst—forms a kind of template in which the surrounding molecules organize themselves into a compound that otherwise would be difficult to construct. This then separates out from the template. Although the new molecule does not really reproduce the template, it possesses somewhat the same structure. A DNA molecule, in a sense, is a template that is able to make another template of the same kind.

In asexual reproduction the whole genetic material of a cell reproduces itself and the cell divides into two cells with identical genetic structures—unless, of course, there is some kind of mutation.

Sexual reproduction is more complex, in which the fertilized egg selects approximately half the genetic raw material from the female cell and about half from the male, and combines them into a new genetic structure, which then starts the creodic process that creates the organism.

Reproductive systems are very important in social organizations. Printing is a good example, where the template—that is, the type—is able to reproduce a mirror image of itself on paper or similar materials many times over. Earlier the copying of manuscripts represented a reproduction. Today records and tapes are reproduced. Because of the existence of language and other means of communication we are able to reproduce images from one mind into another, although never, perhaps, with perfect accuracy. Mutation frequently happens as a result of a failure of reproduction in which the reproduced structure is not identical with the originating one. Oral transmission of language is particularly subject to this, as in the game of "Russian gossip," where somebody whispers a phrase at the beginning of a circle that goes all around the circle and frequently emerges quite unrecognizable at the end.

Social organizations bear some resemblance to biological organisms, in that they exhibit cybernetic, creodic, and reproductive systems, although they also have some properties that are very different from those of organisms. An organization could almost be defined as a set of roles tied together with lines of communication, and sometimes with material flows between them. There is homeostasis in role occupancy. As a person retires, is promoted, or is fired from a particular role, another person is usually selected to occupy the same role by promotion from below or new hiring. Thus a college has freshmen, sophomores, juniors, and seniors, and at commencement the seniors graduate, the juniors become seniors, the sophomores become juniors, the freshmen become sophomores, and then a new set of freshmen is admitted. The structure of the college remains despite the throughput of individuals. Organizations tend to be organized in a hierarchy of roles with complex power and reciprocal relations between successive ranks. Information tends to enter the organization at lower ranks and is filtered out as it goes up through the hierarchy. This filtering is necessary to prevent information overload in the higher ranks, but it also can easily become pathological, as power tends to corrupt the information systems around it with the superior in the hierarchy receiving that information which the inferior ranks think would be agreeable, rather than what is true. Role replacements may also have pathological features. A promotion comes about by pleasing superiors, which is not necessarily closely related to competence and performance of the higher roles. Here again, a dismal theorem—that the skills that lead to the rise to power often unfit people to exercise it—may be seen in operation.

Demographic Systems

Once we have reproductive systems we get populations. Biological organisms are a familiar example. A population is a set of similar objects that may not be identical but are similar enough to create a useful classification. A biological population of organisms is added to by birth and subtracted from by death. Within a given area, population may be added to by inmigration and subtracted from by outmigration. The individual members of a population may be characterized by age. The age distribution—that is, the number in each age group of the population—is an important property of most demographic systems. The dynamics of populations rests on the truism that all members of a given age group will be either one year older or dead this time next year. If age-specific birth rates and death rates are constant, the population can be projected into the future with considerable accuracy. In practice, however, these parameters are rarely constant and nearly all population predictions have been wrong because of this. In the human population, for instance, nobody predicted the great bulge in the birth rate in the United States and other Western countries in the 1950s or the great decline in the late 1960s. Nobody predicted the enormous decline in infant mortality in the tropics that followed the introduction of malaria control around 1950. An equilibrium population is one in which the birth and death rates are equal so that there is no growth and in which the age-specific birth and death rates are constant so that the age distribution is also constant and is actually the same as the survival distribution—that is, the number of each cohort of births that survives in the subsequent years. This situation, however, is rare.

Ecological Systems

An ecological system is a number of interacting populations of different species in which the birth and death rates of each population are a function of its own size and the size of the other populations with which it is in contact. In a given environment of other populations, a particular population may have an equilibrium population. It is then said to occupy its ecological niche. If the population is below equilibrium level, then things will be fairly easy for it: Food will be easy to get, predators may be avoided, births are likely to exceed deaths, and the population will grow. As it grows, however, things get a little harder: Food becomes harder to obtain, space may be more limited, fewer from each cohort of births will survive, death rates will increase, birth rates may possibly diminish (although that may not happen) until finally birth and death rates are equal and the population is stable and in equilibrium. Under circumstances that are not uncommon, we get an ecological equilibrium in which all populations in the system are approximately stable. A pond, a prairie, or a forest that has reached what is called its "climactic state" is found not infrequently in nature. This equilibrium is frequently stable for relatively small disturbances. If we take 25 percent of the fish out of a pond, in a few years the population will rise again to its equilibrium value. The system will pass through fluctuations of related populations of diminishing intensity.

The three most important cases of ecological interaction of two populations are as follows: (1) *Mutual competition:* the more of **A** the less of **B** and the more of **B** the less of **A**. This may have an equilibrium but is rather precarious, and slight changes in the circumstances may easily lead to the extinction of one of the populations, sometimes called the "principle of competitive exclusion." (2) *Mutual cooperation:* the more of **A**, the more of **B**; the more of **B**, the more of **A**. This also can lead to equilibrium, which, however, can be fairly stable. (3) *Predation*, of which parasitism is a special case, in which the more of the predator, the less there will be of the prey; the more of the prey, the more there will be of the predator. This also turns out to be a fairly stable situation.

Human artifacts form an ecosystem along with biological artifacts or organisms. Automobiles and horse carriages were mutually competitive. With a few exceptions, the automobile eliminated the horse carriage. Automobiles and gas stations are mutually cooperative, and they have both flourished. In a small way automobiles are predative upon people in terms of accidents, although they may be mutually cooperative in terms of transportation. The great difference between biological organisms and human artifacts is that each biological organism contains the genetic structures that can produce another similar organism, either within itself, as in asexual reproduction, or in sexual reproduction within two organisms of opposite sexes. The genetic structures that produce human artifacts, however, are not embodied in the actual artifacts themselves (at least until we make self-reproducing machines) but are spread around a large number of human minds and other human artifacts.

Evolutionary Systems

Ecological systems continually change under the impact of mutations—that is, changes in the parameters of the system. This produces an evolutionary process that can be defined as ecological interaction (which is selection) under conditions of constant change of parameters (which is mutation). Mutation can take the form of genetic mutation, creating new kinds of organisms and biological systems, or new kinds of human artifacts in social systems through invention and discovery. The concept should be expanded, however, to include environmental parameters like climate and soil change. The evolutionary process on Earth does seem to exhibit a directionality toward complexity, especially toward greater cybernetic systems in organisms, the development of mobility, the senses, nervous systems, and perceptual apparatus, culminating in human consciousness. The reason for this directionality is not altogether clear but is probably related to the fact that ecological systems will tend to have empty niches for species at higher levels of complexity than those now existing, which will eventually have some probability of being filled by mutation.

Human Systems

The process of biological evolution eventually produced the present human race some 50,000 to 100,000 years ago. With this remarkable development evolution goes into a new gear and the world system is profoundly transformed. Humans may share a good deal of their genetic equipment with the chimpanzees, but the genetic difference between us and the chimpanzees, however small it is, is of overwhelming importance and carries us over an evolutionary watershed into a different kind of world. This is because of the capacity of the human nervous system for extraordinarily complex images and for language and communication, which enables us to have images in our minds of places, times, and structures as big as the universe or as small as the quark, which we have never directly experienced. This is something no other biological organism is able to do, and it has created a whole new system for the world in terms of human artifacts. The landscape over large parts of the Earth's surface has been transformed by human artifacts—cities, farms, roads— although there are still areas of wilderness. Even these are penetrated by hikers and climbers with boots and equipment, and even the South Pole now seems to be surrounded by human garbage. We even have garbage on the Moon, and boats and submarines sail the seven seas. There are more species and subspecies of human artifacts than there are biological species, and they tend to be the dominant species in a great many of the world ecosystems, like cities. Increasingly, even biological organisms are the result of human intervention, first by selection (which produced Pekingese dogs and prize cattle), now by genetic intervention with recombinant DNA. The human race has also changed the energy throughputs of the world system through agriculture and through the burning of fossil fuels and, more recently, the release of nuclear energy.

In spite of our capacity for consciousness and for knowledge, the human organism is still something of a mystery to us. We certainly understand much more about its physiology and diseases than we did earlier, and the process of learning about this still goes on at a rapid pace. The human brain, however, still remains a mystery. It is a system of perhaps literally inconceivable complexity with as many neurons as there are stars in the galaxy and an uncountable variety of possible states. A brain with only ten billion neurons is considerably smaller than most human brains. With each neuron capable of only two positions (it is certainly capable of more than that), the number of possible states of the system would be $2^{10 \text{billionth}}$ power. This is a number that would take us 90 years to write down at the rate of one digit per second, and while the number of actual different states of the brain in the course of a lifetime is certainly less than that, it is still an uncountably large number. We do not know how many different states of the brain there are in each second when we are trying to solve a difficult problem, but it is probably very large. We know very little about the physical, electrical, and biological structures by which the images of the mind are coded in the brain. This means also that the human learning process is profoundly mysterious. It involves inputs of information that are coded in some sense into the structure of the brain, but we do not know the extent to which the engram, the structure of memory, is coded electrically or even molecularly. The great neurophysiologist, Karl H. Pribram (1983), compares the brain to a hologram. Large parts of its structure seem to be coded with enormous redundancy, perhaps in each cell. What releases the hologram we do not know.

The problem of the relation between the brain and the mind is an old philosophical conundrum and still far from being solved; it may not even be solvable. We have an increasingly complex image in our mind of the brain, and we have also in our mind an image of the mind itself, an immense complexity of images of places, times, structures, conditions, and relations that are accessible to us in the process of search, which, again, is little understood. There are also parts of the mind that are inaccessible to us, except by procedures such as psychoanalysis. There are almost certainly parts that are completely inaccessible to us but that influence what is accessible, such as stored memories that are inaccessible to us but that may influence our images and our behavior.

Our image of the brain and our image of the mind are so different (although they are very clearly related) that it is not surprising that humans have frequently conceived the mind as, in some sense, independent of the brain or the body, capable of an existence without it, even though the evidence for this is hard to come by. There is much evidence that the structures of the mind are coded or mapped in the brain, or perhaps even in other parts of the body, or in the body as a whole, but we know very little about how this is actually done. Certainly the mind can be changed by brain operations, even by chemotherapy. We know a little bit about the chemistry of emotions, but very little about the chemistry of thought. What we have to contend with is that each human being is a complex mixture of predictability and unpredictability. It is a system that is capable of extreme positions, even though these may be rare, but they have to be reckoned with.

One of the most tantalizing and unsolved problems of human systems is what so often seems to arrest the learning process. I have compared the limitations on human learning to a vast hall, the walls of which are the genetic limits. Nearly all of us paint ourselves into a small corner of it and fail to realize our genetic potential for learning. We know all too little about how this happens.

Social Systems

Social systems arise out of the interactions of human beings and their artifacts. They are foreshadowed among nonhuman biological organisms going back to the termite colony and the beehive, the beaver colony and the wolf pack. Bees seem to have something of a language that enables one bee to tell another where the best honey is. Termite architecture, impressive as it is, seems to depend on the structuring of fairly random processes of building. Beaver colonies and wolf packs may have a leader that can communicate with the rest and even develop a little division of labor, but compared with these, social systems of human beings represent orders of magnitude of greater complexity. Social systems arise fundamentally out of the imaging quality of the human mind and the capacity to transfer very complex images from one mind to another. They also involve complex mutual learning processes, not only from language and communication but also from experiences, which also communicate. Social systems also involve evaluations, for all choice-directed behavior involves the evaluation of alternative images of the future.

The state or position statement of a social system consists of the mapping of all the human beings in it, each one itself an organization of great complexity, described only partly by such indicators as age, sex, color, shape, knowledge content, skills, and so on. In addition, we should map all human artifacts and even relevant objects not made by humans. These consist of things: material objects, furniture, clothing, houses, factories, automobiles, machines, and so on. They also include organizations, which are a little harder to map. Each one consists of a structure of relationships among people and things, and as we move into process, the change in this structure from one moment to the next, one day to the next, one year to the next. Like the succession of frames of a movie, we can detect patterns in the relationship, for instance, of production and consumption. Every person and object ages and eventually dies or is consumed, and these populations may be replaced by new births or productions.

Production involves the coming together of many different kinds of human beings and material objects, constant communications, organizational hierarchies, and so on; orders that are obeyed or disobeyed, information that may change images of the future and subsequent decisions, and so on.

To reduce this great buzzing confusion into some kind of order, we have to have classifications, and it is a difficult problem to determine what classifications are most useful. For some purposes, for instance, the common classification by gender, race, nationality, and native language may be less significant than classifications by even such simple things as height, beauty, and membership in communication networks. A rough classification of the nature of interactive relationships among persons is into threat relationships, exchange relationships, and integrative relationships, which include such things as identification with a community, persuasion, legitimacy, love, hate, and so on. Threat relationships (you do something I want or I will do something you do not want) are particularly important in political structures. Exchange relationships (you do something I want and I will do something you want) are particularly important in economic relationships. Integrative relationships (you do something because of who you are and I am or what we both belong to) are important in the arts, religion, family, social groups, and organization. All organizational structures participate in all three of these relationships, though to different degrees.

The evolution of social systems, like all evolution, involves a learning process by which we learn how to produce increasingly complex objects, organizations, and people. Processes of mutation and selection are at work here, as they are in biological evolution. The concept of an empty niche, which may or may not be filled by a mutation, is very useful. Just as Australia had an empty niche for rabbits, most parts of the world have had an empty niche for automobiles, even for Mc Donald's hamburgers, for new religious sects, for universities, and so on. The social system is so interconnected that any division of it is a little arbitrary, but, as we shall see, we can conveniently divide it into the economic system, the political system, the communication system, and integrative systems.

Beyond social systems we cannot rule out the possibility of what might be called "transcendental systems," which the religious experience of the human race especially has hinted at. It would certainly be presumptuous to suppose that systems complexity ended at the level of the human race. Just as an ant has very little conception of the human system that may be hovering over it, except perhaps a dim perception of something large and perhaps dangerous, or a dog perceives us as a benign deity and not as another dog, so we may stretch forth intimations of what is beyond us. Certainly our ideas about the transcendent have had a profound impact on human and social systems.

Note

1. The word is from the Greek word meaning steersman. It is the K in Phi Beta Kappa, philosophia bios kybernetica, philosophy the steersman of life.

CHAPTER 2

The World as a Physical System

We distinguish three broad levels of complexity in the systems of the world and the universe: physical, biological, and social. These stand also in order of the time of development. The physical universe was here certainly long before life. It took about 3 billion years on this planet for the first forms of life to develop into the human race. Only human beings are capable of forming genuine social systems, although we do have something that looks like them in the termite colony, in the beehive, and in the social animals, like wolves, baboons, and beavers. Each set of systems forms the environment for the one that follows it. Underlying both biological and social systems is a physical environment, which limits both the structures and the processes of biological and social systems. Underlying social systems is both a physical and a biological environment.

It would take many volumes even to begin to describe what we know about the physical system of the earth, and a brief chapter can do no more than outline the major features. We look at the physical system, however, particularly from the point of view of being a limiting environment circumscribing the development of both biological and social systems. There may be aspects of the physical systems that are not particularly relevant to the biological and social systems. It is those aspects that are relevant to which we will mainly devote our attention.

Virtually all systems consist of components, or parts. These are subsystems, the relationships among which constitute the larger systems. Whether there are ultimate particles in the universe that have no parts we do not really know. Modern physics certainly suggests that there are a considerable number of elementary particles, the internal structures of which, if they exist, have certainly not been discovered. These elementary particles build up, among other things, protons and electrons. These in turn build up the chemical atoms: hydrogen, carbon, oxygen, nitrogen, and so on. The chemical atoms build up structures that are compounds, or molecules. When they reach the complexity of DNA and its derivatives, these structures have the property of building up living organisms. Living organisms increased in complexity, culminating at the moment in the human race.

The human race has a remarkable capacity for producing artifacts, both complex physical and chemical structures that have never existed before—even the transuranium elements that may never have existed before, except perhaps momentarily in an early stage of the universe. Now we are making biological genetic structures that have never existed before. The human artifacts also include social organizations and structures, and, to a large extent, the learned content of human minds. The teacher is a craftsman making images in the minds of the students, with their help, just as a shoemaker makes shoes with the help of leather.

Underlying all physical systems are the broad concepts of matter, energy, and information. These are all interrelated; as we know all too well in the nuclear age, matter can be transformed into energy, or perhaps it is more accurate that some of the energy that is bottled up in the atom is released when an atom is split and "dies" and is transformed into other atoms. The chemical properties of atoms—that is, what other atoms they can hitch onto to form compounds—are closely related to the number of electrons that are associated with a given proton. The solar system analogy here, with the proton as the sun and the electrons as the planets, is much used, although it can be misleading. Another analogy is that the chemical compound is a bit like a multiple star controlling the electrons of several protons. Another metaphor is that the elements have outstretched hands carrying magnets that can be either positive or negative. When a positive hand meets a negative hand, the hands are clasped. Carbon has four positive hands, hydrogen has one negative one, and when each of the hands of carbon hitches onto a hydrogen we get CH_4 (methane). It is perhaps no accident that CH_3 is called a radical, because it is unsatisfied. It has a free hand looking for another hand. Oxygen has two negative hands, which can easily hitch onto two of carbon's hands; the other two can hitch onto another oxygen to make CO_2 (carbon dioxide). The carbon monoxide is a little puzzling here, which may be why it is so lethal. Carbon hitching onto itself in long chains (and sometimes in circles, as in benzene) opens up the possibility of enormous complexity in molecular structure, which eventually led to DNA and to life. Crystals form when atoms hitch onto each other in a regular three-dimensional pattern. Salt, for instance (sodium chloride), crystallizes in a network of cubes, each of which has a sodium and a chlorine atom at each end of an edge.

The Earth has a history of chemical evolution, just as it does of biological or social evolution, although we do not know much about this because the record is so fragmented and is constantly being destroyed by geological upheavals. Both physical and chemical evolution are strongly influenced by energy environments, especially the temperature and the pressures that gravitational and possibly other forces create. A great many substances can exist in three forms: solid, liquid, and gaseous. Substances are solid when the temperature is low enough so that the jiggling of the atoms does not disrupt their spatial pattern, whether this is a crystal or an amorphous substance, in which the patterns are irregular but still stable. As the temperature rises, the molecules jiggle more and at the melting point become a liquid to which, for instance, a pailful of fine sand approximates in some of its properties, where the molecules slide around each other but do not form permanent structures. At higher temperatures the jiggling of the molecules and the atoms reaches a point where the liquid boils to gas, and the molecules are much further apart and are able to have trajectories in space, occasionally hitting each other. Any molecule will disintegrate if the temperature becomes high enough. At very high temperatures the atoms themselves disintegrate.

A great deal of the complexity in the physical world, therefore, is simply a result of warming up, cooling off, spreading out, and clumping together. The physical structures and processes that are essential to life seem to be able to exist and function only within a narrow range of temperatures and pressures. Life certainly cannot exist below the freezing point of water. It seems to function best at around our own blood temperature. It does not seem to be able to function at all above temperatures well below the boiling point of water. We know less, perhaps, about the limits of pressure, although these certainly exist. There are also limits imposed by the availability of different elements. It does not look as if life can exist without carbon, hydrogen, oxygen, and nitrogen, which are the major components of DNA, proteins, carbohydrates, and fats, among other things. There also seem to be quite a number of other elements that are necessary, such as calcium for bones. There are also a good many elements that seem to be necessary in very small quantities—potassium, magnesium, sulphur, and so on. Whether under other physical conditions complexity can develop with other sets of elements we do not really know. Silicon, for instance, which also is quadrivalent like carbon, is a bit too big to arrange itself in complex patterns, but it has been suggested as a possible basis, and it is perhaps significant that it is so important in "Silicon Valley" in computers.

There is a principle here that I have sometimes called the "Goldilocks Principle," after the famous nursery story in which Goldilocks found the father bear's porridge too hot, the mother's too cold, and the baby bear's just right, so she ate it all up. Venus is certainly too hot for life. Life cannot develop at a temperature above 400 degrees, which seems to be about the temperature of the surface of Venus. Mars we are not quite sure about. It may have been too cold or too dry for life, which seems to require water, although there is considerable evidence that in previous times Mars had much more water than it has now. The Earth, however, was clearly "just right"—the right temperature, the right atmosphere, the right amount of water, the right soils, the right elements—to sustain life. It looks as if it is an improbable planet from what we know of the others in the solar system, and it is difficult to tell what the probability of something like the Earth developing in other parts of the universe may be. One factor of importance is that it had to be just the right size. If it was much smaller, it would not have held an atmosphere, as the moon did not. If it was much larger, it would not have cooled off fast enough, like Jupiter and Saturn. It also had to be just the right distance from the sun to create the range of life-sustaining temperatures. We tend to take the physical system of the Earth very much for granted, when actually it is a most remarkable and implausible system, and we should regard it with some degree of surprise and even wonder.

The earth is certainly a total physical system when we look at its overall history. Again, this is a wonderful example of D'Arcy Thompson's Law (1952)—it is what it is today because it got that way. On the other hand, like all systems beyond the most elementary, it is made up of parts, and the parts, certainly over considerable periods, can be relatively independent of the rest of it. The atmosphere comes closest to being a total world physical system. It is a great heat engine, powered by energy from the sun, which warms up the equator much more than it does the poles. The sun evaporates water from the seas and the inland waters, also from plants, especially forests, and this water eventually falls to the surface as rain, snow, or hail. The water vapor at colder temperatures condenses into clouds, droplets, or snowflakes, from which it is precipitated.

Clouds are surprisingly complex structures, whose physics and chemistry we still do not understand well. It certainly looks as if raindrops or snowflakes have to nucleate around small particles of solid matter (dust), but cloud seeding—that is, scattering particles from an airplane that could act as nuclei for raindrops—has turned out to be very disappointing. It is quite doubtful now whether it has any effect.

The larger pattern of the atmosphere is fairly simple; pressure and temperature decline, for instance, as we go away from the Earth's surface. But the detailed structure is astonishingly complex, with clouds, storms, hurricanes, tornadoes, and so on, which are microsystems within the larger atmospheric system. Yet the processes by which they originate and even move about are still imperfectly understood.

Meteorologists are trying to solve these problems by large-scale computer modeling, but modeling is useful for prediction only if the parameters in the real world are stable. The search for a celestial mechanics of the atmosphere may turn out to be very frustrating. There may be, for instance, what I have called "watershed systems," where some configuration of the environment produces a situation in which very small causes can produce very large effects. Thus on the Continental Divide a chance event—a puff of wind, an exclamation from a hiker, the flick of the tail of a mountain goat—can send a drop of water to one ocean or another thousands of miles distant. Storms build up, for instance, by a complex set of processes, some of which involve positive feedback. The more clouds there are, the easier it is for new ones to form, and so on. If a storm builds beyond a certain point, it becomes a hurricane, or it develops tornadoes. Eventually, of course, the negative feedback processes take over: The rain falls, the clouds get smaller, the storm eventually disappears. We do know that the path of storms is related to the position of the jet streams that circulate the poles, but these streams are also constantly shifting. What determines this shift we still do not really know.

We have to think of the atmosphere as a process, something like the overall process of evolution, even though its general structure does not change very much. But the detailed changes—that is, the weather—depend upon when events of varying degrees of probability actually happen. Thus the atmosphere, which seems like such a relatively simple system, actually turns out to be almost as complex as economics; indeed, the record of prediction of economists and meteorologists is highly comparable. I am not sure, but economists may do a little better.

Another very large system is that of the oceans. This is not such a unified system as the atmosphere because of the way in which at the present time the continents divide the oceans, even though they are united around Antarctica and to a much smaller degree through the Bering Strait and the passages from the North Atlantic to the Arctic Ocean. The Atlantic Ocean and the Pacific Ocean, however, are relatively isolated systems. This is illustrated even by their organisms. For instance, the ecosystem on one side of the Panama Canal is markedly different from that on the other side. It has obviously had a history of several million years of divergent evolution after the North and South American continents were united by a land bridge.

There is much that we do not know about the pattern of vertical circulation in the oceans, particularly things like the diffusion of carbon dioxide, what happens to the stuff that is washed out from the continents, and so on. The pattern of ocean currents has been of great importance to the human race. Without the Gulf Stream, for instance, Western Europe might be almost as uninhabitable as Laborador. Pacific currents off the coast of Peru are also of great importance. Recently these have been much disturbed and we have seen the "El Nino" phenomenon, in which the nutrition-bearing water from the deeper oceans failed to penetrate the coastal waters, so that there is an enormous decline in fish and the birds that eat the fish, with severe economic deprivation for the fishermen who depend on the fish for their livelihood.

A very important aspect of the Earth's physical system is the tides, caused by the shift in the gravitational field as the Earth and the Moon revolve and, to a smaller extent, as the Earth revolves around the sun. Because tides are almost part of celestial mechanics, they are highly predictable, much more so than the weather. The configuration of particular coastlines, as in the Bay of Fundy or the Irish Sea, affects the tides substantially, and this creates a few minor human problems. The existence of tides may have had a significant effect on biological evolution, although it is hard to demonstrate this. It seems likely, however, that the intertidal area between the high and low tides has been a fertile place for the formation of new species, and it could well be that if the Earth had not had the Moon it would have been much more difficult to make the transition of life from the oceans onto land, although we cannot be sure of this.

When we come to the land masses, we see the Earth as a single system over the long-term historical perspective, but as a set of very diverse and virtually unrelated systems at any one moment of time. Plate tectonics, which is now the accepted doctrine in geology, following some remarkable evidence from the mid-Atlantic basaltic upthrust, has made clear the fact that by some process the Americas were being pushed away from Europe and Africa. There is evidence that the continents were originally separate and then came together in a single continent (Pangea) and then split up again around the central core of Africa. The Americas floated off to the west, pushing up the Sierras and the Andes in the process. Europe floated off to the north, with Spain pushing up the Pyrenees; Italy, the Alps; and the Balkans, the Carpathians. India floated off to the northeast, pushing up the Himalayas, and Australia floated off to the east and Antarctica to the south. The Red Sea and other rift valleys are current stages of this continuing process.

We still do not understand this dynamics very well. The Colorado Rockies, for instance, are a little hard to account for. And there do seem to be several little chunks of continent that have wandered around the Earth quite a bit, for instance, to form a good part of California. This is the theory of terranes. Whether there are any accidental or random factors in this process, of course, we do not and probably cannot know, but it certainly seems to be hard to get a deterministic model for it.

Thus we see the physical shape of the Earth's surface—its mountains, rivers, plains, oceans—as the product, as we saw in the last chapter, of the constant interplay between the entropic processes of erosion and the filling up of lakes and oceans, and the destruction of mountains, offset by the anti-entropic processes of plate tectonics and, we should add, vulcanism. Volcanoes certainly increase the average height of the land

surface above sea level. It is a fascinating and perhaps irrelevant reflection, incidentally, that when a stone rolls downhill it does not change the
average height of the land above sea level, unless it rolls into the ocean.
Vulcanism is clearly related to plate tectonics. Most of the volcanic areas
of the world are places where the underlying crust is being pushed under
a continent, as we see around almost the entire rim of the Pacific. There
may be some exceptions to this, like the Hawaiian Islands, which seem
to be the result of a kind of traveling spout of lava, now active only in the
Big Island. However, there are some puzzles. The quiescence of the
Pyrenees, the Caucasus, and the Rocky Mountains, seems a little out of
character. Earthquakes, of course, are closely associated with vulcanism
and are an inevitable accompaniment of the "cracks" along which the
continents divide, but it is difficult to get much of a time perspective on
this. Volcanoes leave much larger and explicit records than do
earthquakes.

As a result of all this instability, the land surface of the Earth has
developed an enormous variety of subsystems—rocks of all ages,
volcanic deposits, soils, deltas, and so on. Every square centimeter
(or even smaller) of the Earth's surface is a little different. The soil of
one farm is different from the soil of the neighboring farm. Each is a
little system of its own, affected perhaps by erosion and wind-blown
deposits from some distance away, but often fairly independent of the
farm next door. The distribution of different kinds of land surface,
along with the distribution of climate, weather, and water, is a very
important factor in dividing the Earth up into habitats for the
biosphere, and perhaps even a greater variety of habitats for the
human race, stretching from the temperate zone to the tropical forests
or to the Arctic tundra.

This variety and the isolation of subsystems, habitats within the
Earth's surface, has been of great importance in the history of
evolution. We see this spectacularly in the Oceanic Islands, many of
which—like Mauritius, New Zealand, or Hawaii—were separated
from the mainlands for many millions of years, so much so that while
the birds were able to get there through flight, the land animals
(mammals and reptiles) could not. Hence, these islands developed
unique evolutionary processes. Even the separation of the different
islands of the Galapagos archipelago (which is reported to have given
Darwin some of his ideas for evolution theory) produced striking
differences in species—especially of finches—even though they were

separated by only a few miles of sea, and the islands have been separated perhaps for only a few million years.

Another factor that has played a considerable role in developing the physical system of the planet has been ice ages. These are still something of a puzzle. Positive feedback processes may have played a role here. Relatively small random fluctuations—for instance, in the solar flux and the amount of solar energy the Earth receives—could have cooled the Earth off a little, which, of course, would produce more snow, which would increase the albedo (that is, more solar energy would be reflected back off the Earth), the Earth would get still colder, there would be still more snow and still more solar energy reflected back, until we got an ice age. It is fortunate that the ice never reached the equator, or the evolutionary process might have come to a sad end, or at least a very severe retrogression. One problem is that each ice age tends to destroy a great deal of the evidence about the last one. Geologists and paleontologists, one feels, are trying to read a library most of which is destroyed every so often. Nevertheless, it is clear that the last ice age we know most about profoundly altered the physical structure of the world and scraped most of the soil off the more northern parts and deposited a lot of it further south, creating great lakes and floods, gouging out mountain valleys. I suspect that ice has a more powerful effect in destroying mountains than does rain, but I am not sure of this.

One thing that is clear about the physical system of the Earth is that it cannot be taken as a constant. Not only are there profound changes going on all the time, originating within the physical system of the Earth and its environment, especially in the solar system, but with the development of biological and social systems, each of these has a profound impact on the physical system of the Earth. The impact of the biosphere on the physical system arises mainly because living systems are open systems, which absorb energy from the sun and use this to build more complex and less entropic chemical compounds—for instance, through photosynthesis. All living systems, furthermore, take in a complicated set of materials from the environment in food or in breathing, or even perhaps absorption through the skin, and they give out a different set of substances in breathing, perspiration, and excretion.

Furthermore, as biological organisms increased in complexity they developed elaborate food chains, so that to assess the whole impact of the biosphere on the physical system of the world we have to look at what goes in at the bottom of a food chain and what comes out at the top. It is really a food network rather than a food chain, and it develops into food cycles in which what some organisms give out other organisms take in, so that the chain, as it were, becomes a circle. The nitrogen cycle is a famous one: Bacteria take in nitrogen from the atmosphere, which they then give out into plants, because the plants are able to take in more complex nitrogen compounds than they excrete, and the nitrogen is turned into proteins and other substances within the plants. When an animal eats the plants, the nitrogen is transferred into more complex proteins and such within the animal body. The animal then either excretes the nitrogen in the form of complex compounds in the excretion (which plants may be able to utilize directly) or else the animal dies, its body decays, and nitrogen returns to the atmosphere (or, again, may be utilized by plants or other animals). We thus have a very complex cycle of nitrogen atoms between the atmosphere and the biosphere.

A similar cycle is the oxygen/carbon dioxide cycle. In the sunlight plants take in CO_2; photosynthesis then makes complex compounds and structures and the plants give out oxygen. Animals, of course, breathe in oxygen and breathe out CO_2. This is a good example of one of many unconscious, cooperative arrangements through which the biosphere has expanded throughout the evolutionary process, both in complexity and perhaps in size. Two species, **A** and **B**, have a cooperative relationship if the more of **A**, the more of **B**, and the more of **B**, the more of **A**. This is much more common in the biosphere than is sometimes thought. The tooth and claw may be visible, but the invisible helping hand may be much more significant in the long run.

Because of its inputs and outputs, the biosphere changes the physical environment in which it lives. Soil is created partly by physical and chemical processes, but to a considerable extent it is created by the microorganisms and the worms and so on that inhabit it. One of the most spectacular impacts of the biosphere on the physical system seems to have been the transformation of the atmosphere from one rich in CO_2 and with very little oxygen into one of nearly 20 percent oxygen that we have now, largely through the operation of the earliest forms of life, which seem to have been anaerobic—that is, they took in CO_2 and gave out oxygen. This might almost be described as the "first great pollution," for it eventually killed off most of the anaerobic organisms, although a few still survive today in odd places. This happened slowly enough, however, so that genetic mutation produced the oxygen-using organisms, which actually turned out to have a greater evolutionary potential, although we cannot be sure of that. Most plants indeed are anaerobic by day, taking in CO_2 and giving off oxygen, and aerobic by night, taking in oxygen and giving off CO_2. This opened up an evolutionary potential for animals, which are almost completely aerobic—that is, they take in oxygen and give out CO_2.

There are many physical processes, of course, on which life has had very little effect. The sea is salt, for instance, simply because there was salt in the earth—I don't know why. Salt is highly soluble in water, so that when it rains any exposed salt will tend to be washed into the rivers and into the oceans. The only exception to this is inland salt lakes that dry up, as we have in Utah. The biosphere, as far as I know, contributed nothing to the saltiness of the oceans. It just had to adapt to it, which it did fairly successfully.

Because of the potentialities of DNA for almost infinite variation, the vast repertoire of mutation has made the total biosphere adaptable to changes in the physical environment. One does not have to go all the way to the Gaia hypothesis (that the biosphere operates almost as a single organism).[1] The biosphere is not a single organism, but it is certainly a system that possesses resilience in the face of change in the physical environment.

The relation between the physical system of the Earth and the social system is even more spectacular than the impact of the biosphere, considering the extraordinarily small time span during which the human race has been in existence. This is because of the extraordinary capacity of the human race for producing artifacts that are cooperative with it, which accounts for its almost continuous increase in population at what seems like an accelerating rate. Humans are, of course, biological organisms and share in the input and output processes of the biosphere, although as purely biological organisms they probably have much less influence on the physical system than, shall we say, the tropical forests or bacteria.

Human artifacts, however, also have inputs and outputs that can profoundly change the physical system of the Earth. Human beings have probably transformed the landscape of the Earth in a very short period far more dramatically than the biosphere has ever done, building cities and roads, draining swamps, building dams and making lakes, turning forests and prairies into farms, and in the process creating enormous quantities of waste. From the point of view of the material structure of the Earth, humans are a highly entropic system, digging up coal and pumping out oil, burning it, mining large numbers of minerals and ores and spreading these in dumps and oceans all over the world. An increase in material entropy occurs when the basic elements become more evenly distributed and when chemical compounds become simpler. The geological history of the Earth through the anti-entropic processes, largely of mountain-building and vulcanism, has created ores—that is, concentrations of particular minerals. The human race has been very busy mining these ores and distributing the materials in much less concentrated forms, in dumps or even into the atmosphere and the oceans. When we burn fossil fuels we take complex compounds and turn them into simple ones, like CO_2, along with a few more complex ones that cause smog.

Meteorologists are worried that the CO_2 we are pouring into the atmosphere from burning fossil fuels, much of which must have been taken out of the atmosphere when the organisms that produced the fuels were alive, will have a profound effect on the climate of the earth. The most common view emphasizes the "greenhouse effect"—that CO_2 in the atmosphere stops very little of the high-powered energy coming in from the sun but does stop the low-powered energy radiating from the earth, at least in part (National Research Council Climate Board, 1983). This means that the Earth's atmosphere, especially at the surface, will warm up. This could produce profound physical changes—for instance, melting of the ice caps. This would produce a substantial rise in the level of the oceans, perhaps by as much as 150 feet if all the ice caps melted. There might also be profound changes in the distribution of rainfall, perhaps turning Iowa into a desert and Laborador into a garden. The political effects of all this would be enormous. It is ironic that while so many meteorologists have been predicting this, the Earth has been cooling off at a rather unprecedented rate in the last 25 years and it is still something of a question as to whether increased CO_2 would not increase the cloudiness of the atmosphere and hence increase the albedo of the Earth, with the Earth reflecting off more sunshine than it does now and hence getting colder.

These problems illustrate the extraordinary complexity even of the physical systems of the Earth and our profound ignorance about the nature of the Earth as a total physical system. It is hardly too much to say that the backwardness of the Earth sciences—especially in terms of long-run effects—is a serious handicap in finding the solutions of certain social problems. It is not, of course, that the Earth scientists are backward. Geology, indeed, has become one of the most exciting of the sciences in the last generation—somewhat, I confess, to my surprise and delight. We have to recognize, however, that when we look at the Earth as a physical system over 3 billion years or more the record of what has happened is extremely imperfect. Geological events, of course, do leave records; otherwise we would not be able to find out anything about the past. But it must be recognized that all we know of the past is from our records of it, whether geological, archeological, or documentary. These records are not only an extremely small sample of the totality of what has happened, but they are a biased sample, biased by durability, for only the durable survives from the past into the present. Furthermore, the geological history of the Earth has been so complex that it is like trying to read a document that has been erased 30 times and rewritten. It is not surprising, therefore, that the long-run changes are extremely obscure.

Nevertheless, the question of the limits of the physical system of the human environment has become increasingly urgent, particularly in light of the current population explosion of the human race. The physical environment is an important element in determining the carrying capacity of the Earth for any particular species, the carrying capacity being defined as that population at which births equal deaths and the population, therefore, is stationary. We do not really know what the carrying capacity of the Earth is for human beings. But if we go on doubling the human population every few decades, as we have been doing, we are bound to reach it pretty soon, whether this is 8 billion, 16 billion, or 32 billion. There is an uneasy feeling that we may have overshot the long-run carrying capacity of the Earth for human beings and that in some parts of the world at least a major demographic catastrophe is in store. For once a population starts expanding rapidly, it is difficult to stop this expansion without some sort of catastrophe, like, for instance, the Irish famine of the 1840s. It has been suggested that the carrying capacity of the solar system for human beings would be enormous—perhaps a billion times the present population—if we moved out into space, with self-repro-ducing space colonies, between the orbit of Mars and Venus, using solar energy and mining the asteroids. At the moment this seems a little fanciful, but it is not wholly absurd, simply because of the very low energy requirements in space.

Just how important the physical system of the Earth is going to be in limiting human activity in the future is a large question that is going to be debated for a long time, one hopes. On the one hand, we have the doomsters, as in the first Club of Rome report (Meadows et al., 1972), who see the exhaustion of exhaustible resources and the pollution of available reservoirs of waste as an urgent and almost insoluble problem, at least over the next few decades. At the other extreme we have the "cornucopians," like Julian Simon (1981) whose faith in the "ultimate resource" of human intelligence is so buoyant that the natural resources are seen as a minor obstacle to human expansion, as indeed they have been for the last 200 years, and the human capacity for finding substitutes for anything that we run out of is seen as virtually inexhaustible.

The truth, as usual, probably lies somewhere between these two extremes. The "ultimate resource" of human learning certainly points to those aspects of the physical system of the Earth that we have not yet utilized. On the energy side, one can be permitted a cautious optimism, in that the Earth is an open system in regard to solar energy and that the solar energy that hits the Earth's system at present is in total enormously more than is necessary to power a world economy much larger than we have now. The problem is, of course, that solar energy is extremely diffuse and that collecting it (for instance, in covering the deserts with mirrors) is space-consuming and could be highly detrimental to the environment. The most promising development here seems to be in photoelectric cells, which directly transfer solar energy into electricity. The sun that falls on the roof of a ranch-type house would be enough to power it. This would probably not be true of an apartment building, so we may turn out to be grateful for urban sprawl. The cost of solar electricity has come down spectacularly in the last ten years, but it is still at least ten times, and maybe more, the current cost of conventional electricity. If it could come down to five times, four times, or three times the current cost, it would not be unbearable, even though falling off roofs would be a serious occupational hazard. Furthermore, if we can do it with silicon, that is certainly something that we are not going to run out of. It is one of the more common elements on the earth's surface.

Other parts of the physical system of the earth are potential energy sources, even though they are ultimately exhaustible. A great unknown, of course, is fusion power, especially from the deuterium reaction. If that problem can be solved economically, there is enough deuterium in the top foot of the oceans to keep us going for perhaps hundreds of thousands of years. The problems of controlling what is essentially much the same reaction that goes on with the sun is a little frightening, and we may not be able to solve the technical problems involved.

Other ways of using solar energy lie somewhere below the horizon, and it is hard to tell if they will arrive. There are methods—for example, OTEC (ocean thermal energy conversion), which seeks to exploit the difference in temperature between the surface and the depths of the ocean (Benoit, 1980). Then there is the possibility that we could substantially improve the capacity of the biomass to absorb solar energy; it now uses barely 1 percent of it on the average. We could grow things to burn, as we have done for a long time, but do it much more efficiently, with new kinds of plants or even algae: suppose, for instance, we developed a super sugar to turn into gasohol.

Perhaps the most cheerful thoughts on this matter, strangely enough, come from economists, and it is odd how economics seems to have become the cheerful rather than the dismal science of this generation. Economists point out that when the relative price of something rises, two things happen: People conserve it and then have an incentive to find new ways of producing it or to find substitutes for it. We see this dramatically in the case of the impact of the rising price of oil on the efficiency of its use, which has been very noticeable. An econometric study done for the National Academy of Sciences Committee on Nuclear and Alternative Energy Systems (CONAES—1980) came up with what for many was the surprising conclusion that a fourfold rise in the price of energy would have no effect on the economy. One could see this even without an elaborate model. Energy in the 1970s was about 7 percent of the economy. A fourfold rise in the price would produce enormous conservation and an increase in energy efficiency, so it would be unlikely to go to 15 percent. This would leave 85 percent instead of 93 percent for other things, and relatively small increases in productivity could offset what looked like a horrendous increase in energy prices. The case for cautious optimism rests.

When it comes to materials, the physical systems gets a little more worrying because the Earth is virtually a closed system in regard to materials. We can neglect the occasional meteorite. It is certainly true that the economists again will say that as the price of materials rises, substitutes will be found, as we have seen recently in the case of copper for electrical transmission. Plastics and microwaves have effected quite a revolution. We see it also in computers, which have become fantastically energy- and materials-conserving. There is a legitimate worry about materials like phosphorus, necessary for agriculture and indeed for all biological organisms, that can only be found in deposits that are being used up and end up frequently being flushed down toilets and out to the oceans, where it is very diffuse and hard to concentrate. We might, of course, find phosphorus in asteroids or even on the moon and mine it, but that seems a long way off, even though it is not absurd because of the low energy requirements in space.

The physical system of the earth and its environment in the solar system may impose some ultimate limitations on the evolutionary process, and this seems highly probable. The sun, after all, will burn itself out in a few billion years, and that will be the end of the evolutionary experiment, if it lasts that long, in this part of the universe. I refuse, however, to let this prospect give me any sleepless nights. I am much more worried about what might happen in the next 10 or 25 years. It is the physical system of the Earth that made the nuclear weapon possible, although it took the "ultimate resource" to realize it. This could bring the evolutionary experiment in this part of the universe to an end very rapidly. And again, the "ultimate resource" of human intelligence is the only thing to which we can look to prevent this. But that we will pursue in a later chapter.

The change in the physical system of the world, closely related to certain changes in the biological and social systems, that presents perhaps the greatest source of concern for the human race at the present is soil erosion. Even before the human race, of course, there was soil erosion from wind, rain, snow, rivers, glaciers, and so on. This is one of the very ancient entropic processes in the material surface of the earth. It is offset to varying degrees by the anti-entropic processes of soil formation. This happens partly through almost purely physical systems, such as the formation of deltas by rivers, the deposition of soil-building materials of various kinds at the end of glaciers and icecaps, and the chemical disintegration of rock that seems to take place at the interface between the soil and the rock that underlies it. There may have been something like soil even before life, but certainly life, once it got out into the soil, transformed it and continues to do so. A good deal of soil-building activity is due to bacteria, worms, roots, animal excretion and decay, and so on.

The human race has introduced profound changes in the soil structure of the planet, especially through deforestation and agriculture. These changes are not all unfavorable. The introduction of the dung beetle into Australia almost certainly improved the soils there. In China there is a long tradition of rebuilding soils from human and animal excrement. Humans probably added lime to soils a long time ago, and of course, in the last 100 years the growth of artificial fertilizers has been spectacular. The end result of all this, however, seems to have been an increase in soil erosion that has much exceeded any increase in soil rebuilding, and the net soil erosion is potentially a very serious human problem. Lester Brown (1984) suggested that this is a problem of the same order of magnitude as the using up of fossil fuels, and we may have even less time to correct this imbalance. This is something, furthermore, we simply cannot afford to lose. Solar energy is at least a potential substitute for fossil fuels. Up to now we know of no substitute whatever for soil. It is not inconceivable, of course, that we might develop a nutritious and rapidly growing algae that would grow in ponds and would not need soil. This is very speculative.

At the moment we are also exhausting the ocean fish resource, which, in a certain sense, is a substitute for soil, but if the oceans are too much overfished—as is happening—we may face a serious decline in food supply from this source even in the next generation. Forests are another worrying problem, especially the tropical forests. The increase in population in many parts of the mountainous tropics has resulted in catastrophic denudation of the forests in search of cultivable land and firewood and a consequent rapid soil erosion under the influence of tropical rains in the absence of a forest cover. There is also a serious problem in the attempt to convert tropical forests into large-scale crop-growing, as in the Amazon Valley, which can easily be disastrous, particularly where there are lateritic soils, which easily turn into rock when the forest cover is removed. The effect of the loss of tropical forests on the atmosphere and climate may also be a serious problem. These questions are not receiving the attention of governments they deserve, yet they may well be the most serious changes in the physical system of the world affecting the future of the human race.

Note

1. See Lovelock (1979).

CHAPTER 3

The World as a Biological System

In one sense the biomass—that is, the aggregate of all living organisms spread over the surface of the globe—has always been a total system, in that it is conceptually capable of description for each moment of its existence since the beginning of life. Again, we could describe it as a "time cube" in which each living organism appears as a kind of thread going through time from its conception to its death. How many living organisms have existed in the last three billion years since life originated on Earth I would not hazard more than a wild guess. If we suppose a million living organisms per square kilometer (and if we consider bacteria this is far too small), an average length of life of one year (which is probably much too large), we get something like 15×10^{23} organisms that have ever lived. To give an idea of the order of this magnitude, the number of stars in the galaxy and the number of neurons in the human brain is about of the order of 10^{11}.

Although all organisms that have ever lived and are still alive constitute in some sense a system in space-time, this is by no means a single integrated system, especially at any one time or over a short time period. It is a vast mosaic of habitats and ecosystems, with virtually all species of living organisms confined to particular geographic areas, some of them very small, like the ecosystem under a rock or in the stomach of an animal. When we talk about areas here, of course, we really mean a volume above and below a particular surface area, for life exists in the soil, for instance, below the surface, at least down to the solid rock, and, particularly after the formation of flying organisms, such as insects and birds, exists in the atmosphere, above the surface, or, for instance, in various levels of treetops or bushes. This is to be understood when we talk about life inhabiting a given "area."

The physical system of the Earth, as we saw in the last chapter, has produced very complex structures, especially in the land mass and even below the level of the ocean, in things like coral reefs and deep warm water jets. Some species of living organisms have been confined to small, isolated areas. Others have spread fairly widely over the globe, especially with the coming of flight and migratory birds and insects. Even walking and crawling animals, of course, can cover large distances in migration, as do plants through their mobile seeds carried by the wind, water, or the digestive system of animals. With the innumerable changes in climate, ice ages, and so on, and with the movement of land masses because of plate tectonics, which has created isolated continents and the Oceanic Islands, both species and ecosystems have shifted their locations around the globe. Nevertheless, most habitats have been fairly small and isolated, although they have been constantly subject to migration. The isolation of ecosystems, as we see especially in the divergent ecosystems of Australia, New Zealand, the Oceanic Islands (like Mauritius and Hawaii), North and South America, and so on, has had a very important impact on evolution, especially by oceans, although sometimes by deserts and mountain ranges. Although we can certainly think of the world as a total biological system over time, at any one time it has tended to be a complex pattern of isolated and partially isolated ecosystems.

With the coming of the human race, however, and even then perhaps for only the last few hundred years, the world has developed for the first time a species that has the whole world for its habitat. There are now virtually no parts of the surface of the Earth or even the depths of the seas, and now even the far planets of the solar system, which either humans or their artifacts have not reached. This is because of the extraordinary physical adaptability of the human race, which can survive even without much in the way of human artifacts in ecosystems as diverse as tropical forests, savannahs, coral islands, and so on, and because even quite early in human history the extraordinary capacity of the human race for producing artifacts enabled human beings clad in furs to survive in the Arctic and with primitive implements and weapons to survive in dense tropical forests.

In the twentieth century we have gone to the poles, to the top of Mt. Everest, to the deepest levels of the oceans, and to the Moon. We have sent our artificial eyes and other senses out beyond Saturn and to Venus and Mercury. This is a profound evolutionary change, the consequences of which cannot be predicted, but it does mean that because of the human race the world has become much more of a total biological ecosystem than it was before. We see this, for instance, in the catastrophic extinctions the human race has produced in the more isolated environments, like the Oceanic Islands, which they have penetrated. Mammals had not been able to reach the more isolated Oceanic Islands, like Mauritius, New Zealand, and Hawaii, before the human race discovered them, although the birds reached them and actually occupied many of the ecological niches that the mammals occupied on the mainlands. Humans, however, introduced pigs into Mauritius, which certainly exterminated the dodo; rabbits into Australia, which at least endangered some native species by their explosive population growth; goats into the Sahara, which may easily have played a role in turning it into a desert; deer into New Zealand, and so on. Furthermore, we now have kangaroos and koalas in almost every zoo in the world.

The origin of life on the Earth is still a mystery. All life as we know it today seems to be organized by the extraordinary molecule DNA, discovered by Watson and Crick a generation ago, so it is at least a plausible assumption that before DNA there was nothing that we could really call life, although there may have been a lot of organic molecules surging around in some kind of primeval soup. Even Crick (1981), however, thinks of DNA as a molecule of such incredible complexity that its production through chemical evolution on Earth has a very low probability. He suggests that it may have come from outer space, although where it could have come from there only throws the problem back a little. Our ignorance of the past, and especially so distant a past as the moment when life began on Earth, is so great that it is hard to blame the creationists for stepping into the breach. When we run into these highly improbable events, as we do when contemplating the process of evolution, it is rather comforting to say that God did it, but this still does not answer the question as to how God did it. What is certain is that it was done—that is, there was a moment on Earth before which there was no DNA and after which there was.

Biological evolution rests firmly on two extraordinary properties of DNA. One is that of self-reproduction. I have described it as the "first three-dimensional Xerox machine." Its remarkable double-helix shape evidently permits it to attract similar molecules and amino acids from its environment, to form a kind of mirror image of itself that is then able to split off and create another mirror image, which is exactly the same structure as the original DNA. It is almost as if our image in a mirrror is able to see itself in the mirror and create a perfect copy of us, although that analogy is perhaps a little farfetched. The exact processes by which DNA reproduces itself are still somewhat mysterious, but there is no doubt that it does reproduce itself.

The other even more remarkable property of DNA is its capacity for forming a structure—a genome—that operates as an organizer, or plan, enabling it to build living organisms, ranging from the simplest viruses to human beings. It is only a slight stretch of the metaphor to call this capacity "know-how." My own fertilized egg "knew how" to build a human being, *Homo sapien,* a male, with light-colored skin, originally with black hair, blue eyes, a pretty fair brain, along with a heart, a liver, lungs, and all the rest. It did not even know how to make a dark-skinned female. It certainly did not know how to make a hippopotamus, even though the DNA that does know how to make a hippopotamus has many things in common with mine—that is, it also knows how to make a vertebrate skeleton, heart, liver, lungs, brain, and so on, but on very different proportions and scale.

It is important to recognize that every fertilized egg contains DNA molecules that are virtually unique to that egg. A possible exception is identical twins, or siblings, which evidently come from a single fertilized egg that splits, so that the DNA in them is virtually identical. DNA is not a single molecule but a pattern of molecules all of which have the same structure, but there are millions upon millions of patterns each corresponding to a particular organism. When a cell divides under normal circumstances, however, the two cells that produce it have identical DNA, whether this is in the asexual reproduction of the one-celled organism, like the amoeba, or whether it is the multiplication of a particular kind of cell within an organism.

The overall process of "morphogenesis"—that is, how the fertilized egg becomes an organism such as a chicken, or even how the recently divided cell grows into a full-sized cell—is still very mysterious. We are beginning to find out something about it, particularly in regard to which portions of DNA correspond to what process in the formation of the organism, but the overall process is still puzzling, particularly how cells differentiate in order to form, for instance, liver cells, bone cells, the large number and variety of different kinds of cells that complex organisms require.

What we do know is that in order to realize the potential of the fertilized egg or the divided cell, DNA must have access to energy. In the case of the growing fetus, this comes from the chemical energy of the mother's body. This energy is necessary to transport and transform the materials that the DNA presumably selects and builds into the very complex structures of the organism. Energy and materials, each of many different kinds under some circumstances, might be called "limiting factors" in the growth of the organism, in the sense that the potential of the genetic structure cannot be realized unless they are in its environment. After birth the DNA continues to organize the growth of the organism into the child and into the adult, and also organizes the aging and eventually the destruction of the organism in death. The DNA that originally gave me black hair also knew how to turn my hair white, or at least did not know how to keep it black.

All living organisms are organizations committed to eventual self-destruction in death. It is a little hard to equate DNA to St. Paul's concept of sin, but there is no doubt that with DNA came death as well as birth. There is some question perhaps as to whether the asexual reproduction of the amoeba, for instance, involves the death of the original organism, although I would certainly argue that once the cell is divided into two, the original cell is no longer there and has, in effect, died. There is no question, however, that with sex came death and that all organisms created by sexual reproduction have within their constitution the necessity of eventual death.

All organisms, however, have not only death but birth, which comes from reproduction. In the case of the amoeba's asexual reproduction, the two amoebas that result from the splitting of the original one literally reproduce the original one in terms of their DNA and general structure. With sexual reproduction, half the genetic structure of each parent comes together to form the new DNA of the child. Virgin birth, which apparently is not wholly unknown, produces a child from the mother's egg that contains the full DNA of the mother, and so the child is genetically identical to the mother. In a fertilized egg, however, half the genetic structure comes from the mother and half from the father, so that the child does not replicate either parent.

It is a little puzzling as to why sex turned out to be such a good idea, especially in light of the extraordinary complications that seem to be involved in getting the two sexes together in fertilization. Every species seems to have a different strategy for this. The advantage seems to be that whereas in asexual reproduction the offspring has the same genetic composition as the parent and hence there is not much variety, in sexual reproduction virtually every member of the species has a somewhat different genetic composition. This means that favorable genetic mutations can spread rapidly through a species. It also means that if two parts of a population of a species become geographically isolated so that they can no longer interbreed, the sheer randomness of mutation will lead to a divergence in the gene pool—that is, the total pattern of the DNA in different individuals—in each of the two species until they eventually become different species. The invention of sex, plus the potentialities of the planet for isolating ecosystems, certainly seems to have speeded up the rate of evolution.

Whether there has been an increase in the rate of development of new species I do not know. Species last much longer than the individuals who compose them, but they still seem to exhaust their potential eventually and become extinct. There are supposed to be several hundred extinct species for every extant one, and the average duration of a species might not be more than about 10 million years. As it spreads over space and time, the biological system of the earth, then, is seen as a system of profound disequilibrium and constant change. Evolution, indeed, depends on the endangerment of species and the succession of ecosystems.

A pattern that dominates all evolutionary processes is that of mutation and selection. Selection takes place both within a species and between species in ecosystems. The gene pool (the total stock of genetic structures of a species) changes constantly as individuals die and are born. In sexual reproduction the gene pool is constantly rearranged as between members of the species. If one member of a species has a mutation in its genetic structure (a mutation is simply a change, which can happen for many different reasons), this may or may not be passed on to the children, for only half the genes of the children come from one parent, although not always the same half. The more children an individual member of the species produces, therefore, the better chance there is that any change in this genetic structure will also be found in some of the children. If these changes are favorable to survival and to reproduction, then the changed DNA will spread throughout the species. This is what biologists call "reproductive fitness." This can happen, for instance, if the change in the gene makes for a better chance for survival of a fertilized egg into adulthood, or if it increases the adult's chances of finding a mate or of producing children.

It seems to be less readily recognized by biologists that a change in the gene structure that is well adapted to spread through the population of the species may not lead to the survival of the species itself in the ecological interaction in the larger ecosystem. Some good examples of this can be found in species that practice strong sexual selection—for instance, where the males fight for the females, or where the females attract the males by some sort of display. This can easily lead to changes in the species that endanger the species itself. A good example could well have been the Irish elk, where the males evidently fought or at least did a ritual battle for the females, and the ones with the biggest horns usually won. This meant that a mutation producing larger horns rapidly spread through the whole population, so that horns got bigger and bigger until all the males got caught in the bushes at an early age and the species died out. On the female side, the bower birds or the peacocks could well be species where sexual selection would drive them to extinction, at least in the wilds.

Ultimately, selection is dominated by processes of ecological interaction that determine whether the population of a species will grow, decline, or remain stable. An ecosystem is a system of interacting populations of different species. A basic concept here is that of the ecological niche, which is an equilibrium population. Biologists are a little inclined to see niches in terms of physical environments, but the most essential definition is that any species that has an equilibrium population will have a niche. If the population is below the equilibrium level, conditions will be rather favorable, it will be easier to find food and easier to get away from predators, and the population is likely to grow. As it grows, however, conditions become less favorable, until at some point deaths rise and births decline until births and deaths are equal, at which point the population is at equilibrium. This equilibrium is frequently cyclical in the sense that the population tends to rise by sheer momentum of growth above the equilibrium level, then falls toward it, then below it, then up above it again, and so on, but unless these cycles are very large they do not affect the system much over time.

The birth and death rates in any given species depend on its total environment, which includes all the other species in the ecosystem. In this sense there are three principal significant relationships between two species, **A** and **B**.[1] There may be *mutual competition,* in which case the more of **A**, the less of **B** and the more of **B**, the less of **A**. This can produce an equilibrium for both species, but it is somewhat precarious. A slight change in the conditions (the parameters of the system) can easily lead to the extinction of one species and the expansion of the other. Two species eating the same food would be likely to have this relationship, like two species of weevils in a bag of flour. However, this is rare in nature. It is very rare for the food intake of two species to be identical. Species may also compete for nesting places or for territory. Here again, the coexistence of competitive species is possible but always a little shaky.

Another not uncommon relationship is that of *mutual cooperation,* where the more of **A**, the more of **B** and the more of **B**, the more of **A**. A striking example is lichen, which is a combination of two genetically separate species, a fungus and an alga, neither of which seems to be able to survive without the other. Some insect colonies have two or more species in a mutually cooperative relationship. Another good example is that of the dung beetle and ruminants, like sheep or cattle. Dung beetles spread the dung over the landscape and so increase the production of grass. The more dung beetles, the more grass and the more sheep; the more sheep, the more dung and the more dung beetles. Darwin gave a delightful example of the relation between domestic cats and clover illustrating the complexity of these relationships: The more cats, the fewer mice; the fewer mice, the more bees; the more bees, the more clover.

The third type of relationship is that of *predation* or *parasitism,* in which the more of **A**, the less of **B**, but the more of **B**, the more of **A**—the more wolves, the fewer rabbits; the more rabbits, the more wolves. Surprisingly enough, this relationship turns out to be very stable for both species, unless (and this can happen) it gets out of hand, in which case it can be disastrous for both species. The predator keeps the population of the victim down to the point where at least there is plenty for it to eat and the population of the victim, of course, supports the population of the predator. Parasitism is similar, except the parasite is usually smaller than the victim whereas the predator is usually larger. This relationship also can be very stable.

As we saw in the previous chapter, the biosphere frequently interacts with the physical system of the Earth in cooperative ways that sustain rather stable systems, as we saw in the example of the nitrogen cycle or the oxygen-carbon dioxide cycle. The persistence of the biosphere depends a great deal on the development of cycles of this kind, simply because organisms require input and output, and if there is no recycling, stocks of input will gradually be replaced by stocks of the output, as we saw in what has been called the first great pollution, in which the anaerobic organisms used up most of the carbon dioxide in the atmosphere and turned it into oxygen, a change they could not survive. With the development of the mixed ecosystem of plants and animals, however, the oxygen given out by plants becomes the input of the animals, which they turn into carbon dioxide, which becomes input for the plants. This is a pretty stable system, although it is quite possible that the end of a carboniferous era came when the plants used up so much CO_2 that many of those that relied on it became extinct.

An important concept for understanding the overall evolutionary process is that of the "empty niche." An empty niche is defined by a species that *would* have an equilibrium population in a given ecosystem, if it existed. An empty niche, therefore, provides an opportunity for either mutation or migration. It is very clear, for instance, that Australia had an empty niche for both rabbits and European-type humans. Once they were introduced, they spread very rapidly, somewhat to the detriment of the original species. When an empty niche is filled, of course, this changes all the other niches in the system. Populations that are mutually cooperative with the species occupying the empty niche will expand, and those mutually competitive with it will contract, sometimes to extinction. Similarly, unless a genetic mutation produces an organism that has an empty niche, it will not survive—that is, empty niches provide the opportunity for successful mutation.

It should be stressed that genetic mutation is not the only kind of change in the system. Climatic changes, soil erosion, and the silting up of lakes and deltas are all mutations in the sense that they change the parameters of the local ecosystem. We can observe this, for instance, in the filling up of a lake. The streams that flow into it deposit more solids in it than the river that flows out removes, and the plants and other species that occupy it perhaps absorb carbon from the atmosphere and leave part of it in the mud and the soils. The lake has a succession of rings of ecosystems, depending largely on the depth of water. Thus it may be surrounded by forests, there may be an ecosystem of swampland or shallow water near the shores, another one for the middle of the lake and the surface, another one perhaps for the deeper parts of the lake, and so on. As the lake fills up and dries out, the forest creeps in on the marsh, the marsh creeps in on the shallow water, the deep water becomes shallow, and so on, until finally the lake turns into a marsh and then into a forest.

This process is known as ecological succession, and it can take place without any change in the genetic structure of the various ecosystems. It sometimes results in what is called a "climactic ecosystem," in which the underlying physical parameters cease to change or change very slowly. A similar process of ecological succession is seen after a forest fire; at first fireweed, then bushes, then perhaps one species of trees, which can be succeeded by another species. The pine forests of the southern United States, for instance, cannot reproduce themselves if left alone because the shade is too dense for the pine seedlings to grow but not too dense for hardwoods to grow, so that the pines are eventually succeeded by hardwoods unless they are either burned down or cut down every few decades.

A fascinating example of cyclical succession is at the boundary of the tundra and the most northern forests. The forests at the northern boundary may shade the soil so much that the permafrost creeps down and eventually kills off the roots of the trees, and the forest then becomes tundra. The tundra, however, has no shade, and so the sun melts the permafrost to the point where the trees can reestablish themselves and it becomes a forest again, after which the whole process repeats itself.

A useful and general definition of evolution is that it consists of ecological interaction, which involves selection—that is, the diminution of some species to extinction and the expansion of others—under conditions of constantly changing parameters, including climatic, physical, and genetic. The fact that we observe these patterns throughout virtually all evolutionary processes does not mean, however, that evolution is deterministic. Evolution proceeds by the filling of empty niches, by changes in the parameters of the system, especially changes in the genetic parameters. Because of the random element in mutation, however, we can only postulate a certain probability that mutation will take place that will occupy the empty niche within a given time. Empty niches, however, do not stay around forever. Changes in other parameters of the system and in other species will eventually close them. The probability that an empty niche will be filled, therefore, before it closes, is never 1.0. If the mutation that could fill the empty niche does not happen before the niche closes, then the whole subsequent history of the Earth will be different than if it does happen.

The actual course of events on Earth has been profoundly affected by the particular dates at which improbable events happened. No matter how improbable an event, it will eventually happen if we take a long enough time perspective, although exactly when it will happen cannot be predicted. There is a parallel here, even in some of the physical systems of the Earth, such as floods. What we call a "100-year flood" is a flood the magnitude of which has about a 1 percent per annum probability of happening. We cannot say when it will happen but the probability of it happening in 100 years is about 63 percent; in 400 years, 98.4 percent; and in 1000 years, 99.995 percent; but when it will happen within these periods we cannot predict. Thus evolution is not at all like celestial mechanics, and the only reason why we can make accurate prediction in celestial mechanics is that the evolution of the solar system has virtually ceased. If nothing is happening, prediction is very easy.

There is a fundamental principle here that the unpredictability of evolution is not just the result of human ignorance to be corrected as we learn more about it. It is inherent in the nature of the system. This is because evolution is a process in information rather than in just matter or energy. Certainly matter and energy are highly significant in evolution, but only as limiting factors. The genetic structure is information coded in matter and at some point perhaps translated into energy as morphogenesis takes place, but the information is what is crucial.

It is important to recognize that the same information can be coded in many different ways. We see this in the phenomenon of human speech, where information structures of great complexity originate somewhere in the brain. These are coded into nervous impulses (mainly electrical) that go to the vocal cords. They are then coded into material vibrations in the vocal cords, which in turn are coded into sound waves, which are energy, although in a material medium. These reach the ear of the listener and are coded into electrical impulses, which then are coded into certain structures of the brain, which we very imperfectly understand, so that an image from the speaker is transferred into the brain of the listener. If the listener laughs at the speaker's joke, the speaker gets feedback that what he said has in fact been transferred, at least in some sense, into the brain of the other person.

It is one of the great discoveries of information theory, however, that information essentially has to be surprising or it is not really information (Shannon and Weaver, 1964). We are not surprised when an eclipse takes place at the predicted moment because fundamentally we are dealing with a mechanical system that is not really an information system. What has to be surprising, however, cannot be predicted. We see this clearly in the old story as to what would happen if we had tomorrow's newspaper. The answer is, of course, that tomorrow would not happen—it would be very different. All the people who were going to have something bad happen to them would take precautionary steps to try and prevent it from happening. Everybody would rush to buy the stocks that were going up and sell the stocks that were going down, so that the stocks that were going to go up would go up far more than the paper asserted, and those that were going down would go down much further, and so on. We should not be discouraged, therefore, if evolutionary theory lacks predictability. This is inherent in the system itself. This is not to say that the system has no patterns. We can make rough probabilisitic predictions of the future, but this is different from the exact predictions of systems, like celestial mechanics, in which the parameters remain constant.

The uncertainties of the evolutionary process are accentuated by the possible role of catastrophes—that is, sudden changes in the physical system of the Earth, perhaps confined to particular locations, perhaps almost universal—that are usually adverse to many existing species and cause large-scale extinctions. The separation of the layers of sedimentary rocks into different geological ages with fairly sharp boundaries between them suggests that each age has ended in a particular location because of some kind of catastrophe. Between the top layer of the rocks laid down in one age and the bottom layer of the next layer that succeeds it there is frequently a large extinction of species apparent in the fossil deposits, followed by the sudden development of many new species, and sometimes a whole new order of living organisms. The geological record has been so distorted by many subsequent catastrophes that for the older records especially we can never be quite sure whether they represent a catastrophe that really happened in the past or whether there has just been some catastrophe in the record itself destroying, say, the intermediate stages between two geological eras. However, there does seem to be a great deal of evidence for real catastrophes in the past, of which, of course, the extinction of the dinosaurs is one of the most spectacular.

The importance of the isolation—that is, the division of the world into relatively isolated and unconnected ecosystems (which are already noted as an important possible feature in the evolutionary process)—may also be significant from the point of view of the incidence of catastrophe. A purely local catastrophe, such as the eruption of Krakatoa, which destroyed all life on Krakatoa Island, will not have any great evolutionary significance if what is destroyed is not isolated but is part of a larger system. Thus the ecosystem on Krakatoa has now, after a hundred years, been largely reestablished by migration from nearby similar ecosystems that were not destroyed. A local catastrophe, however, that destroys an isolated ecosystem that has evolved differently from other parts of the world certainly lessens the total gene pool of the world, and this might have significance for the future when the isolation diminishes and contact is established between the previously isolated ecosystem and the rest of the world.

There is also a possibility that catastrophe might create isolation. A succession of ice ages, for instance, may do something like this, both by destroying and creating islands as the sea level rises and falls, or by isolating patches of arctic ecosystems in the tops of mountains, which in the previous ice age had been united with the arctic system. The tundra in the high Rockies, for instance, is very similar to the tundra of northern Canada, even though separated by hundreds of miles of quite different ecosystems at lower levels.

A difficult question to answer, but one that cannot be avoided, concerns the impact of the size of ecosystems on the rate of successful mutation. In a large, uniform ecosystem there may not be so many empty niches as in smaller, more isolated ecosystems, and hence the rate of evolution will be slower. Mutations of great importance for the future may be successful and survive in small, protected niches in relatively isolated ecosystems when they might not survive in larger ecosystems. One of the real puzzles in evolution is the survival of the early developments in structure, like the eye, or even the brain, which turn out to be very successful later on but which could have great difficulty surviving in their early stages. This is a little bit like the so-called infant industry argument for protection in economics—that a new industry could not survive foreign competition when it was small but would be able to do so as it grew. If it is destroyed while it is small, of course, it will never grow. There is even something like this in the way in which the long period of childhood and growth into maturity in the human race is protected by the rather isolated ecosystem of the family.

A very interesting question is whether biological evolution has a direction, a "time's arrow," and, if so, why? The record suggests there are at least three directionalities in evolution over time. Perhaps the most obvious and the most fundamental is the movement toward complexity. This is difficult to measure, except in a rough, qualitative way, but I am sure all human beings are convinced that they are much more complicated than the amoeba, even more complicated than the chimpanzee. This increase in complexity looks like a steady process from the viruses to the cell, from the one-celled organism into the many-celled organism, from the external skeleton of the insects to the internal skeleton of the vertebrates, from the sluggishness of the reptiles to the liveliness of the birds, and the growing intelligence of the mammals, culminating, of course, in us.

A distinct aspect of this growth in complexity is the development of control systems that protect and insulate the organism from its environment, particularly from unfriendly aspects of its environment. We see this even in the development of mobility, as we move from plants to animals, although single-celled organisms may actually have more mobility in proportion to their size than do plants. The many-celled organisms, like plants, may actually sacrifice some mobility for complexity in structure and size.

Another aspect of control is the development of the senses—sight, smell, hearing, touch, and taste—using a wide range of coders of information: light waves, sometimes stretching beyond the human capacity into infrared or ultraviolet, sound waves, pressure indicators in touch, and chemical indicators in smell and taste. These almost have to go along with the development of interpreters in the nervous system of these information inputs, which translate them into some kind of "knowledge" of the environment, and also some kind of image of space, without which sense data are not much good. There also have developed not only passive sense data but also the alarm cry and the song of the bird, the howl of the wolf—even, perhaps, the chemical emissions of the tree, which are sensed by other forms of life, especially in the same species. The colors and scents of flowers are also a part of this pattern to attract insects as agents of fertilization.

The culminating development of complexity is the development of primitive knowledge structures and sensitivities into consciousness and awareness of the environment; in human beings, far beyond the immediate environment. This involves also an awareness of the self and of the mind—that is, the consciousness of our images of ourselves and of the world. This includes the development of structures within the organism that have some kind of one-to-one correspondence or mapping with the total environment of which the organism itself is a part. This begins, perhaps, as a simple awareness, the way the dog is aware of the rabbit it is chasing, and the rabbit of the dog that is chasing it. In the human race this awareness expands to awareness of the whole universe.

Just why the evolutionary process should have these "time's arrows" is by no means clear in ordinary mutation-selection theory. One can speculate, indeed, that in a constant physical environment natural selection would develop a set of organisms and an ecosystem in which the repertoire of possible mutations would become increasingly adverse. This would lead, in time, to a genetic equilibrium in which all mutations were adverse and would not survive, so that the existing genetic structure would be extremely stable. The ecosystem of scientific images in human minds is a little bit like this. Something like this seems to happen toward the end of each geological age where the rate of evolution seems to slow down. This suggests, again, the possible importance of catastrophe in sustaining the evolutionary process toward complexity and the prevention of the development of evolutionary equilibrium at what we might regard today as a low level. Catastrophe destroys an existing genetic equilibrium and opens up new niches for potential mutations that previously would not have survived.

This still does not explain very satisfactorily why there seems to be such a constant tendency toward increasing complexity. A possible suggestion is that any ecosystem is likely to have more empty niches at the top of the scale of complexity than it has at the bottom. The less complex niches will have been filled earlier. This might suggest that catastrophe had a less important role than was suggested earlier, and that as the niches for more complex organisms are filled by mutation, this opens up new niches for still more complex organisms, and a relatively continuous process that has no real need of catastrophe. These considerations have some significance for societal evolution as well.

Another question of considerable interest in the overall pattern of evolution is whether there exist certain general patterns of niches in ecosystems that can be filled in rather different ways. This is suggested, for instance, by the phenomenon of the food chain, which suggests that all ecosystems have to have fairly simple organisms that can transform basic elements in nonliving substances (nitrogen from the air or elements in the soil) into living structures, which become food for more complex organizations, which then become food for still more complex organizations, and so on up the food chain. Even on a certain level of the food chain we may find niches for organisms of different sizes and somewhat different habits.

The development of the isolated ecosystems of the world, like the Oceanic Islands and even Australia, suggests that there are similar patterns in different systems. Thus in Australia the kangaroo occupies a niche somewhat similar to the deer on the other continents; the koala is a little bit like a squirrel; the bandicoot is a little bit like a rat; the wombat perhaps something of a badger; and even the duck-billed platypus a kind of otter. There are 200 varieties of gum trees, also in some sense parallel to the varieties of the trees of the other continents, from cathedral-like forests, which remind one a little of the redwoods, to the snow gums of the higher altitudes, which remind one of the tortuous contours of trees at the higher altitudes of other continents. Even more striking were the ecosystems of the remote Oceanic Islands before humans arrived, where the birds seemed to occupy many of the niches that the mammals did on the continents, even to the extent of having burrowing birds in New Zealand. The flightless birds (the dodo and the moa) occupied what might almost be described as "mammalian niches."

All this suggests that what the biologists called "fitness" is a very complex concept. Here some of Darwin's metaphors were not very appropriate. The "survival of the fittest," a phrase he actually borrowed from Herbert Spencer, as his contemporary Thomas Huxley pointed out, means very little. If we ask "Fit for what?" the answer is "Fit to survive," so all it means is survival of the surviving, which we knew anyway. The crude kind of "social Darwinism" that identifies fitness with toughness and competitiveness is a gross misunderstanding of the complexities of the system. The survival strategies in ecological interaction are very diverse. They consist of finding a niche—that is, fitting into the system. "Survival of the fitting" would be a better analogy than "survival of the fittest."

Similarly, Darwin's "struggle for existence" is an unrealistic metaphor. There is actually very little struggle in the biosphere, except perhaps in sexual selection, where the males fight for the females. As pointed out earlier, this often leads to the extinction of the species. When in an ice age the tundra advances on the forest, there is no struggle between them, only differential rates of birth and death of different species. Biological evolution, then, is a profoundly nondialectical process. It does not proceed by any kind of conscious struggle or by winning fights. It proceeds by differential patterns of adaptability to changing environments. In biological evolution it can truly be said that the meek—that is, the adaptable—inherit the Earth, and that the tough—the well-adapted to a particular environment that are resistant to change—are wiped out when the environment changes.

One aspect of biological evolution that has been somewhat neglected by the biologists is the distinction between biogenetic mutation—that is, changes in the structure of the genes and DNA—and what I have called "noogenetic" change—that is, learned structures in organisms that are transmitted from one generation to the next by a learning process (Boulding, 1981: 14). These learned structures are, of course, structures in biogenetically created nervous systems or brains. Biogenetics creates the potential for these learned structures, but this potential can be realized only if there is a learning process in the course of the life of the organism. There is considerable evidence for learning in birds; there is some slightly more dubious evidence for it in the planaria and in bees. It becomes increasingly important as we get to mammals. There is a famous group of macaque monkeys in Japan that developed a "Newton," who invented all sorts of useful kinds of behavior which she then taught to the younger monkeys, who then transmitted it to successive generations. There we have substantial changes in behavior without any change whatever, as far as it is known, in the biogenetic structure.

When we come to the human race, noogenetic change is overwhelmingly important. The biogenetic structure of the human race seems to have changed very little in the last 50,000 years as far as we know, but human knowledge has increased enormously, as has the human capacity for making artifacts as the result of this increase in human knowledge. The learning processes involved here are of several kinds. There can be rote learning, which simply copies or imitates the behavior of another. There can also be conscious learning, which increases a person's understanding of the universe.

Biogenetics is highly Mendelian, in that the life experience of the organism—that is, the phenotype—is unlikely to affect the genetic structure and will not be passed on in genetic structure to the next generation. The only exception to this would be mutations, caused by exposure to radioactivity, for instance, and it is certainly conceivable that if the general level of radioactivity rose, as it may well do because of human activity, biogenetic mutations as a result would increase the resistance of organisms to radioactivity, as these mutations would have survival value.

When it comes to noogenetics, however, evolution is extremely Lamarckian, in the sense that it is precisely the experience of the organism in the learning processes that is passed on to the next generation. This does require, of course, a biogenetically produced capacity for learning in the nervous system, but there is nothing in biogenetics that says this capacity has to be utilized in the absence of a learning environment. Language is a good example. Biogenetics produces in the human race a capacity, or potentiality, for language. What language or languages are learned, however, has absolutely nothing to do with the genes, but only with the learning experience. There is certainly no gene for the English or the Japanese language, and it is quite rare for a human being not to have the capacity as a newborn for learning any of the thousands of languages or pronouncing any of the hundreds of spoken sounds that the human race has produced. Sociobiologists are certainly right in pointing out that the behavior of organisms is as much a product of the evolutionary process as is their form and structure. They do tend to overlook, however, the enormous importance of noogenetics in the evolutionary process.

The future of the biosphere, now that it has produced the human race, is very uncertain. Humans represent a real "system break" in the evolutionary process because of their enormous capacity for learning, for knowledge, the resulting know-how, and for the production of human artifacts. There are probably now more species of human artifacts all over the planet than there are biological species. The total mass of human artifacts, in terms of buildings, roads, bridges, automobiles, airplanes, furniture, and so on, may well be substantially larger than the biomass—that is, the total mass of all living organisms—although I have seen no estimate of this. Furthermore, human artifacts are frequently competitive in the total ecological system with biological organisms, especially if we include the domesticated biological organisms, such as agricultural crops and domestic animals, as human artifacts.

The human race represents for the rest of the biosphere, therefore, an evolutionary catastrophe, potentially even on a larger scale than some of the catastrophes of the past. We have already caused the extinction of large numbers of biological species and are likely, even in the course of population increase and economic development, to exterminate many more. Such catastrophes are not unknown in the history of the Earth and may well have happened many times in the last three billion years of life. The continuation of the evolutionary process in spite of or perhaps even because of these catastrophes is remarkable. One does not have to go as far as James Lovelock's "Gaia hypothesis"—that the whole biosphere is a kind of organism with a great capacity for adaptation. This is a dangerous metaphor, for ecosystems are not organisms, and the biosphere is an ecosystem of organisms, not itself an organism. Yet the biosphere does seem to have exhibited at various times of crisis a capacity for adjustment and resilience under changing circumstances, which is somewhat analogous to that of the higher organisms, especially in terms of modifying its own physical environment.

Lovelock (1979) suggests that "Gaia" might come to an end with the sun's warming, which would create a physical environment on the Earth with which the biosphere could not cope. An even more urgent catastrophe is in the offing because of the positive probability that exists in the present international system of nuclear war in X years. This could be an irretrievable catastrophe for evolution on Earth, perhaps sending the biosphere back to grass and cockroaches because of the destruction of the ozone layer, as Jonathan Schell (1982) suggests. Or even worse, as Carl Sagan (1983) suggests, the dust from nuclear destruction might cover the Earth and prevent all sunlight reaching it for perhaps three or four years. This would be somewhat parallel to the catastrophe that exterminated the dinosaurs, at least according to one theory, when the Earth was hit by a large asteroid, which again created an enormous dust cloud. This situation would be complicated, of course, by a substantial increase in overall radioactivity on the Earth's surface from the fallout, which would have strikingly differential effects on different forms of life.

On a more optimistic note, the "sociosphere" of all human activity and artifacts also has a certain Gaia-like quality, with a great deal of resilience and learning capacity in new situations. The "noosphere," as Teilhard de Chardin calls it—the interacting sphere of all human knowledge as it spreads over the Earth—comes closer to being an organic cybernetic system than does the biosphere, simply because of its remarkable capacity for communication. The structure and behavior of a kangaroo in Australia has remarkably little effect on that of a polar bear in the Arctic, but a new idea produced in a human mind anywhere in the world has the capacity of spreading all around the world in a remarkably short time, thanks to radio, television, and so on. There is therefore a reasonable hope that the human race will learn how to deal with the nuclear threat and, indeed, with the generally pathological character of the threat system. Then human knowledge leading to genetic engineering might even lead to a great proliferation of new biological species and an enormous increase in the gene pool of the biosphere as part of the system of human artifacts.

Note

1. See Boulding (1981: chap. 4) for a graphical exposition of these principles.

The World as a Social System

Social systems are an evolutionary development out of biological systems involving biological organisms that have powers of communication, consciousness, and an ability to produce artifacts. There are prehuman primitive social systems—colonies of bees, termites, ants, beavers, wolf packs, troops of monkeys, and so on—but it is only with the human race that social systems become dominant. Many species of prehuman organisms produce artifacts—beehives, ant nests, beaver dams, birds nests, and so on. Before the human race there was even some development of primitive tools—a bird holding a stone in its beak, or a sea otter breaking open shells with a stone—but these seem to have been governed mainly by instinct—that is, behavior that is built into the organism by the genetic structure. Bees seem to exhibit some learning in the dance by which incoming bees transmit information to outgoing ones about where the nectar is, and, as we have seen, noogenetic evolution—learned structures transmitted from one generation to the next—is found in many forms of life.

Nevertheless, it is not just human arrogance that persuades us to think that we are different, and that with the development of the human race evolution moved into a higher gear and enormously accelerated. This is perhaps a little surprising in view of the fact that the genetic difference between, for instance, humans and chimpanzees does not seem to be very large. The genetic difference, however, seems to be one of these cases where, in the famous phrase attributed to Engels, "an increase in quantity produces a change in quality." However small the difference between the human brain and the chimpanzee brain, it is a difference that goes over some kind of watershed into another kind of system, simply because of the human capacity for language and for creating images far beyond immediate experience. It would be difficult to describe Antarctica to a chimpanzee and more difficult to explain celestial mechanics.

Perhaps the most visible evidence of this watershed is the enormous proliferation of human artifacts, the genetic structure for which, essentially, is know-how in the human brain. Nobody, as far as I know, has tried to calculate the number of species of human artifacts, but it almost certainly exceeds the existing number of biological species. Virtually all these species of human artifacts have been developed in the last 10,000 years, and perhaps half of them in the last few decades.

The world's human social system, what has been called the "sociosphere" by analogy with the "biosphere," consists of a succession of states of the world social system. The state or condition at any moment in time consists of all living human beings, the contents and the structure of their bodies and minds, all human artifacts, plus the relevant physical and biological environment, plus the interactions among all these things, which are revealed as one state of the world succeeds to the next in time. Here again, the social system is a movie, each frame of which is a state of the social system. Human artifacts include not only material artifacts, from the first eoliths, flint knives, and arrowheads to the space shuttle, but also include human organizations, from the primitive hunting-gathering band to the Federal Reserve System, the Catholic Church, and the United Nations.

The learning process by which the current state of all human beings has been developed is also a human product. Each individual human being is partly a biological artifact, from the know-how in the genetic structure of its fertilized egg, and partly a social or human artifact, through the learning process from other human beings—parents, teachers, and so on—and from other human artifacts, like books and television. There is also an important internal learning process in which human beings help to create themselves. The interactions among all these units are also a part of the picture and, again, are very complex. They include such things as feelings, passions, love and hate, interests, or indifferences. They also include actual exchanges between individuals or among organizations, grants or gifts (one-way transfers), threats and the carrying out of threats, and so on.

Just as the biosphere is a shifting mosaic of ecosystems, each in its own habitat but with some interaction among them, so the sociosphere, until very recently, has been a mosaic of societies, some isolated, most of them fairly self-contained but with some contact with others. There is a good deal of evidence that the human race originated in Africa and spread around the world from there. As it spread, certain genetic changes took place, creating the minor differentiations that we call "race." It is not surprising, for instance, that mutations of darker skin should have had survival value in the tropics as a protection against the cancerous effects of sunshine, and that in the cloudy northern regions pale skin, which took advantage of the vitamin D-forming capacities of whatever little sunshine there was, should have had a greater survival value. With the coming of clothing, suntan oil, and vitamin pills, these biological differences become much less significant, and it would not be surprising if the human race becomes much more homogeneous in regard to skin color over the next few thousand years, but this will not be a very fundamental change.

For the first 40,000 or perhaps 100,000 years of the human race—depending on when we put the beginning, which is by no means certain—paleolithic hunting and gathering cultures prevailed. Whenever population pressure was felt in a group, which could happen in two or three generations if the food supplies were favorable, some members of the group would go to more distant areas where conditions were easier. The human race seems to have had a remarkable capacity for going places and not coming back. Because regular contact under these circumstances was confined to a fairly small area, cultures, and especially languages, became very different. Paleolithic societies produced an enormous number of different languages. There are supposedly some 700 in Papua New Guinea because of the nature of the mountainous terrain, which divided the human population into a large number of isolated groups with only occasional contact (Encyclopedia Brittanica, 1983: 738). Similarly, there seem to have been about 200 or more American Indian languages, each representing a group that split off and remained isolated for a considerable period. The band or tribe in this period may not have contained many more than a hundred people before splitting or having some members migrate.

With the coming of agriculture, the domestication of animals, and settled village habitats, we have a paradoxical situation that the actual mobility of most human beings may well have been reduced. Hunters and gatherers were apt to travel over a much wider range than farmers, but the rather steady surpluses of storable food produced by agriculture permitted the development of much larger societies and civilization, which, as the word indicates, is what happens in cities. Thus while most of the population may have stayed on the farm, a certain proportion of the people, perhaps not more than 10 percent, became more mobile in the form of officials, tax collectors, armies, and traveling priesthoods. Civilization in the classical sense comes from a surplus of storable and transportable food, and the development of some kind of organized threat system to take this surplus away from the farmer and with it feed soldiers, potters, weavers, builders, officials, priests, and scribes who lived in the cities and traveled between them.

Trade played an increasingly greater role in this system, particularly with the development of rivergoing and even seagoing boats, and the domestication of transport animals like the horse and the camel. It is surprising, however, what a large area the Incas and the Aztecs covered in their empires without these conveniences. It is a little surprising that the early American civilizations developed in the mountains rather than on the Mississippi or the La Plata, but tropical rivers, like the Amazon and the Congo, always seem to have been too difficult a habitat to support early civilizations. Nevertheless, it is no accident that the major early civilizations were on navigable rivers—the Nile, the Euphrates and the Tigris, the Indus, and the Huang Ho. There were also what might be called archipelago civilizations on inland seas—the Greeks and the Romans, the early Indonesians, and Japan.

It is significant that both agriculture and civilization seem to have originated independently in at least two or three parts of the world. There is no clear record of any contact between the early American civilization and the Old World. There is not much evidence of early contact between the civilizations of the Far East and those of the Near East and the Mediterranean. This suggests that the human race possessed in its brain a learning potential for both agriculture and civilization that was realized independently in some places but not in others, perhaps because of accidents of physical environment, leadership, and social opportunity.

It is only in the twentieth century that the world has become something like a single social system. Certainly before Columbus, Cortez, and Pizarro, the world was not a single social system at all. The Mayan Empire could collapse in the ninth and tenth centuries without this affecting either Charlemagne in Europe or the Emperor of China, for neither of them ever heard about it. Even up to the middle of the nineteenth century Africa was called the "dark continent"—it had contacts with the rest of the world only in the coastal areas. The Chinese in the Ming voyages actually "discovered" Africa some 50 years before the Portuguese did. Before the sixteenth century contact between China and Europe was quite minimal, confined to a little silk trade on the overland route, and even contact between China and India was somewhat sporadic, although the spread of Buddhism certainly suggests that it was not unknown 2500 years ago. Japan, after initial contact with the Jesuits in the sixteenth century, went into virtual isolation in the Tokugawa period (after about 1618), maintaining contact with China and with Europe only through a handful of merchants on an island in Nagasaki Harbor. Nevertheless, even this period demonstrated the difficulties of isolation, for the "Dutch learning" crept into Japan all through this period, and after Admiral Perry's "black ships" and the Meiji Restoration in 1868, Japan emerged into the modern world almost like a butterfly from the chrysalis of the Tokugawa regime.

In the twentieth century, however, the mapping of the world has become virtually complete. Even when I was a schoolboy there were white places on the globe where nobody had ever been. Now we have not only mapped the globe, but Mercury, Venus, Mars, Jupiter, and their moons. Even today we still find small hunting and gathering bands in remote mountains, as were recently found in the Philippines, who have not had previous contact with the rest of the world, but these are now very rare indeed.

As a result of the rise of science and its application to the production of human artifacts, we have now developed what might be called a world "superculture" from which it is very hard to escape. All airports are similar and seem to be differentiated only by the gift shops and some signs in the local language, and even in the gift shops most of the gifts seem to have been made in Hong Kong or Taiwan. All international airline pilots speak roughly the same language, a derivative of English (which, however, almost deserves to be called "pilot"), as they communicate with airport control towers. Going in from an airport to the city, there will be taxis and buses; approaching the city, whether it be Nairobi, Singapore, Cairo or Delhi, one will see a skyline of skyscrapers, and the city will have electricity, telephones, automobiles, gas stations, hotels, television, department stores, and factories. A few miles outside the city, of course, we may be back in an earlier world of villages and rural poverty.

There are, of course, some exceptions. The communist countries have a certain Victorian charm. It is a curious paradox, indeed, that the more radical the government, the more conservative seem to be the results. Bucharest reminds one of Paris of 1910, with the exception of an Intercontinental Hotel skyscraper in the best neo-brutal modern style. Stalin's taste in architecture was very much that of the Chicago skyscraper builders of about 1900. Warsaw, as rebuilt from the ruins of the war, is a charming medieval and nineteenth-century city with the Stalin-Baroque skyscraper in the middle, and so on. India keeps out Coca-Cola but has a substitute of its own. Beijing, outside of the forbidden city and a few earlier remains, looks much like a nineteenth-century European city. Tokyo, of course, is full of McDonald's, Colonel Sanders, and pizza parlors. Even Tahiti is half Mormon.

Nevertheless, underneath the world superculture is a great variety of local cultures and communities—linguistic, national, regional, occupational, religious—and class cultures, almost all of which have some interactions with the world superculture, and occasionally with each other, yet which have retained their strong sense of identity and perceive themselves as different from the rest of the world. Very few people really think of themselves as world citizens. The national state, indeed, has become an almost universal pattern with the breakup of the old empires—British, French, Dutch, Belgian, Portuguese, American, and Japanese—mainly since World War II. The United Nations grew from some 60 member nations in its inception to over 160 today. There are a few relics of empire, like the Falkland Islands, Hong Kong, still loose spheres of influence like Francophone Africa, the British Commonwealth, the United States' sphere of influence and military allies, the Russian proteges (Cuba, Angola, Mozambique, Ethiopia, Vietnam), and so on, but these connections are rather loose. The Soviet Union and the People's Republic of China are the only two nineteenth-century empires left, with the possible exception of Ethiopia on a much smaller scale, and both Russia and China would almost certainly be considerably better off if they disbanded their empires, and if Tibet and the thirteen or so Russian republics were independent countries in the United Nations. There is, indeed, a "cognitive dissonance" here. It is almost a dialectical contradiction. If Poland can be an independent country in the United Nations, why cannot Lithuania, Latvia, Estonia, Uzbekistan, Armenia, and so on, all of which have long histories of national identity? The evidence is strong that empire was an economic drain on the imperial powers and a psychological and political burden on the colonies (Boulding and Mukerjee, 1972). Certainly Britain, France, Belgium, the Netherlands, and now probably Portugal benefited economically from the abandonment of their empires and had a much higher rate of economic development in the last 30 years than they did in the imperial days.

Many of the new national states and some of the old ones are quite heterogeneous when it comes to regional, religious, and class cultures. Homogeneous nations, like Norway, Sweden, and Denmark, are relatively rare. Nearly all of the new African nations are extremely heterogenous in terms of language, culture, and religion. For the most part their boundaries are accidents of empire, established through the geographical ignorance of the Conference of Berlin in 1884. Nevertheless, they do seem to be developing some kind of national identity, often under great difficulties. Thus the cultural divisions that stretch from the Sahara to the sea in a series of bands running east and west across nearly all the West African countries give them all somewhat the same kind of heterogeneity, from the desert dwellers and Moslems in the north, to the forest dwellers in the middle, and the seacoast dwellers to the south, who have often been Christianized. Nearly all the African countries have many different languages, tribes, and religions. Egypt has Islamic Arabs and a Coptic ancient Egyptian minority. The Sudan is Arabic and Islamic in the north, tropical forest tribal and Christian in the south. Even the *lingua franca* of the bureaucracies and the upper classes, often dating from imperial days, might differ. In Cameroun, for instance, it is half English and half French.

As a result of the two world wars of the twentieth century, the European countries are a good deal more homogeneous than they were in the days of Austria-Hungary and the Turkish Empire. Britain has the Welsh, the Scots, and the disgruntled Irish; France has the Bretons, some Basques, and a somewhat disgruntled Provencal South; Italy has Austrians in the Tyrol; Spain has some very disgruntled Basques; Canada has neither linguistic, religious, economic, nor cultural unity; Iran (again almost an empire) has Kurds, Afghans, and a variety of people; Rumanians occupy a doughnut with Hungarians in the hole; and so we go on. Even relatively homogeneous Japan has half a million Koreans and an enormous variety of religious sects.

When we look at class cultures and occupational cultures, the variety becomes even greater. Everywhere in the world rural people have a somewhat different culture from urban, the more so in the more recently urbanized countries, less so in countries like the United States, where there are still rural subcultures in Appalachia, New Mexico, and parts of the South but where the rural culture of the Middle West, for instance, is hardly to be distinguished from the urban culture. The Iowa farmer is a professional, quite frequently with a college degree, with the *New Yorker* magazine on his livingroom table. In cities all over the world there is a professional class culture of bureaucrats, lawyers, doctors, engineers, and so on, who are college and university trained and are the carriers of the world superculture.

Universities, indeed, are a large part of the genetic structure of the superculture and are remarkably similar all over the world. There is virtually no country without at least one—no matter how small it is—and what is taught, especially in the natural and biological sciences, is much the same everywhere. In the humanities, of course, Russian universities have very large departments of Russian and Russian literature; French universities French and French literature; and so on, which is not surprising. Also, history will usually be taught with a nationalistic or ideological bent. Even so, universities have become much less parochial and more world-minded in my own lifetime. At Oxford in the 1920s anybody who wanted to study

Arabic, Chinese, Japanese, or Swahili would have been regarded as rather strange. Greek and Latin and Greek and Roman history were still "greats," but today if somebody wanted to study Japanese, Chinese, Arabic, or Swahili, they could very well be preparing for a business career. What has happened in the twentieth century has been a tremendous erosion of the "exotic."

The middle classes around the world are more diverse than the "jet set," more nationalistic, more prone to regard anything outside their own country as foreign and exotic, but still much more aware of world problems and of the world as a total system than they would have been 100 years ago.

There is virtually no such thing as a "working class," especially on a world scale. The "workers of the world" do not unite, and probably never will. Class war is a rare phenomenon and totally devastating when it occurs, such as in Cambodia, in the Cultural Revolution in China, and in the First Collectivization in the Soviet Union. There are innumerable cultures among those who work for a living, even among those who work for wages. It is not only that rural cultures are frequently different from urban, for within the urban working class there are enormous cultural differences between, say, the "disreputable" working class and the "respectable," usually churchgoing, working class. There are also great differences in a country like the United States in the cultures of the different ethnic groups, and great differences in the various religious cultures. Jehovah's Witnesses are very different from Irish Catholics, and even Irish Catholics from Mexican Catholics. Politically, political parties in democratic countries tend to be loose alliances of diverse cultural groups.

Within the world of organizations there are also great divergences. Multinational corporations differ from each other as much as churches do. Occupational cultures often are more homogeneous than class cultures. Both workers and employers in the trucking industry are much more alike than truckers are like teachers or office workers.

Another possible distribution of the human race is into interest groups. We could hypothetically divide people into those who are favorably affected, those who are unfavorably affected, and those who are unaffected by any particular change, such as a law, a dam, or a new investment. But is is very hard to identify these interest groups. If we could identify them we would find them very surprising. They would not correspond to any of the visible groups in society, except in rare cases. The most easily identifiable interest groups are occupational groups. Virtually all people in the copper industry will be favorably affected by a rise in the relative price of copper and unfavorably affected by a decline. Included in this group, however, also will be storekeepers, lawyers, municipal workers in copper mining towns, and so on. People who use copper will be adversely affected by a rise and favorably affected by a fall in the price. In the long run, a fall in price will chase people out of the copper industry to other places where they may do even better. There will be complicated impacts on rents and property values, so that even occupational groups are hard to identify. Classes are extremely unlikely to be interest groups. Within virtually any visible class or group, some people will be affected favorably and some unfavorably by any change.

In spite of the great complexity of the diversity of subsystems within the sociosphere, it is certainly legitimate to look at the sociosphere as a totality, even though we can comprehend it only imperfectly, and to ask: How is it different today from what it was yesterday, or even from what is was an hour ago? This difference is the dynamics of the system—that is, change in its state. Then we have to ask ourselves: What are the sources of such change? This is, of course, a large and complex question, but we can give some kind of rough answers. Some changes, of course, may come from the physical and biological environment. There may, for instance, be natural disasters, like volcanic eruptions, earthquakes or floods, or even plagues and epidemics, which affect the sociosphere. These, however, are fairly rare.

If we think of the sociosphere as consisting of populations—that is, stocks of human beings and all other things relevant to them—change comes from birth (or production) and from death (or consumption). Thus with a human population of about 4½ billion, at the present time about 125,000 people die every day from ordinary causes and about 335,000 babies are born, for a total increase of about 210,000. Every person who was still alive yesterday and is still alive today is one day older and will have aged a little, however imperceptibly, and may also have changed in other ways, will have learned something or forgotten something, will be in better health or in worse health, and so on. The same principles are true of the populations of all human artifacts. Thus between this time yesterday and this time today, something like 75,000 automobiles may have been produced in the world, and perhaps (this is just a guess) 30,000 scrapped. Similar estimates could be made for all other human artifacts and commodities. Since this time yesterday a certain number of firms have gone bankrupt and others have been started; laws have been passed, people have been elected to office or resigned from office; within the labor force, so many people have been hired and so many have been fired; and so on. We may be able to estimate how much the price level has risen or fallen. But we have to be careful of these aggregate figures, because each represents a complex reality. It matters, for instance, where people die and are born, where automobiles are produced or scrapped. These considerations will be pursued further in the next chapter.

Many unmeasurable—even unidentifiable—changes may still be important. Are we moving toward or away from war? What new knowledge has come into being in the research community? Has a new prophet or a new political leader started on a career? Who is gaining influence or losing influence? Who is being converted to what? What ideas are spreading and what are retreating? What is becoming fashionable and what unfashionable? It is clear that we are facing an extremely complex, but by no means incomprehensible system.

Looking beyond the mere description of what is happening, we are also very curious about how it happened. What are the underlying processes and principles that turn the state of the world yesterday into the state of the world today? A somewhat different and perhaps more provocative way of stating the same question is to ask: Given yesterday, how could today have been different? If we are complete determinists, of course, we would say that today could not have been different. As we have seen, however, systems involving information, know-how, knowledge, and learning, have strong elements of indeterminacy in them, although there are many elements that are deterministic. We may look, first, at what might be called the "underlying limits" of the system. Given yesterday, what could today *not* be like? That is, what are the impossibilities of the system? If there are constant rates of change or constant rates of rates of change, as there are in the solar system, the system is highly deterministic. Even if rates of change themselves change, these changes will lie within a limited range, and this range limits what today can be like, given yesterday. Thus in terms of population, the rates of change do change, but they change slowly. It would be extremely unlikely to have, say, 500,000 added to the population since yesterday, even less likely to have none, unless there is some unprecedented catastrophe.

The assumption that rates of change will not change or, more subtly, that rates of change of rates of change will not change is the basis of all projections. We have to be cautious about these in social systems, because rates of change do change, often quite suddenly and dramatically. We saw this in regard to human population around 1950, when, as a result of the widespread development of malaria control, we had a sharp reduction in death rates in a great many tropical countries in the space of a year or two. This reduction was quite unexpected and upset all previous projections of population change. Again, the decision of the Chinese government to adopt a rigorous population control policy had a profound effect on the rate of change of Chinese population fairly suddenly.

One of the great differences between the sociosphere and the biosphere is the much greater importance of *decisions* in social systems in determining the future. Decisions are not unknown in the biosphere—as, for instance, in sexual selection, where the females may choose one of a competing group of males to mate with. These choices, however, are usually simple, and human choices are very complex and often affected by random factors. Even when we select from a restaurant menu we may be tossing mental coins and choosing what comes up heads. We run into difficult problems here because what happened in the last 24 hours may depend on a decision that was made six months or even ten years ago, although we could say that such previous decisions are part of the capital stock of yesterday.

A very important relationship is habit—that we do today what we did yesterday. This is a great stabilizer in biological as well as social systems. It is said of weather prediction that we will do just about as well as the meteorologist if we say that the weather tomorrow will be the same as it is today, and this principle has a good deal of validity in social systems. On the other hand, today is never quite the same as yesterday. Change always does take place and is inevitable.

The greatest source of change in social systems unquestionably is the process of human learning, both the development of new knowledge and know-how that the human race never had before and also the spread of old knowledge around to new minds, which is done informally in the family and formally in schools, universities, and other educational agencies. This learning process is very complex. It does not consist merely of the imprinting of immediate experiences on the memory, although this is part of it. It does not consist merely of rote learning of something that can be repeated without really understanding it, although this, too, is part of it. We have to learn a good deal of language this way, and we certainly learn to speak a language as a child without understanding any of the principles of its grammar or evolution. Then there is learning by feedback, which goes on all the time, even in "folk learning." We make a remark and we know that somebody has understood us by their response, or has not understood us by their lack of response or their inappropriate response. We go to where we think our friend lives and find the house empty and have to inquire where he has moved to. We soon learn that if we touch a hot stove we will be burned. Scholarly and scientific learning involves much the same principle of learning by feedback, except that the feedback is somewhat sophisticated and is interpreted in terms of some abstract theoretical image of the world.

The social system can be divided into three large, overlapping, and interpenetrating subsystems, which are distinguished by different modes of interaction of human beings, usually assisted by various artifacts, each of which has a certain rationale of its own that is also part of the human learning process. These three systems I have called the *threat system,* the *exchange system,* and the *integrative system.* All actual human institutions and relationships involve mixtures of all three in varying proportions. A threat system originates when A says to B, "You do something I want or I will do something you don't want." It could be stated in negative terms; "You refrain from doing something that I don't want and I will refrain from doing something that you don't want." The law is often couched in these terms. What happens then depends on the response of the threatened party, **B**. At least five broad classes of response can be distinguished. The first is submission or acquiescence, in which **B** does what **A** wants him or her to do. Second comes defiance, in which **B** refuses to do what **A** wants him or her to do and **A** then has to decide whether to carry out the threat or not, or make new threats. A third possibility is flight, in which **B** can simply run away out of the reach of **A**'s threats. This has been quite important historically and accounts for a lot of the spread of the human race over the globe. A fourth possibility is counter-threat: **B** says to **A**, "You do something nasty to me and I will do something nasty to you." This may lead to deterrence, in which neither threat is carried out, or it may lead into breakdown and the carrying out of the threats. It may also lead into a progressive increase in the threats, as in an arms race. A fifth possibility is threat reduction, in which **B** makes himself or herself a suit of armor or hides in a castle or bunker and so diminishes **A**'s ability to carry out the threat. Legal action is often of this form. Threat systems, of course, are particularly important in political relationships, in the law and criminal justice, and in taxation. Most people pay their taxes because the state or political authority threatens them with various unpleasantness if they do not. And, of course, the threat is overwhelmingly important in war.

An exchange system begins when **A** says to **B**, "You do something I want and I will do something you want." Or "You give me something I want and I will give you something you want." If **B** accepts—and **B** usually has a veto—the exchange takes place. **A** gives something to **B**, **B** gives something to **A**, which may be some physical object, like money or a commodity, or it may just be behaving in some way that is agreeable, like making love or voting the right way. Exchange is the main instrumentality of economic life, as we shall see. It is also present a good deal in political life, in legislative logrolling, in political bargains of all kinds. It is found also in the family and, indeed, in virtually all human relationships that involve some sense of reciprocity. In any relationship there is a sense of what is given up and what is received, and if these are not in some sense equivalent, there will be dissatisfaction with the relationship.

The integrative system is a looser concept, harder to define, and may involve many different concepts. It involves such things as legitimacy, status, a sense of identity, morality, community, affection, and, at the other end of the scale, illegitimacy, enmity, community breakdown, and the like. Legitimacy is a particularly important concept here. I have argued that if we are trying to find any single dynamic system on which the rest of society hangs—and I am not at all sure that we should even try to find such, for society is so interrelated—legitimacy is a good candidate, simply because if any system, practice, person, or organization loses legitimacy, either in its own eyes or the eyes of others, it becomes virtually impossible to continue functioning.

There are, of course, many forms and sources of legitimacy, and its dynamic processes are actually very puzzling. Just why some things lose legitimacy—which sometimes they do quite suddenly—as others gain it is a real puzzle, but it is an essential part of the social system. Without legitimacy—that is, widespread acceptance—governments cannot function. Terrorists are soldiers without a government, for they are usually regarded as illegitimate by others, but they must regard themselves as legitimate or they could not continue to function. Exchange cannot function either without legitimacy. Exchange always involves property, for what is exchanged has to be the property of the exchangers before it can be exchanged. Property, however, has a certain implicit threat behind it, and unless it is legitimated, exchange cannot take place. Thus slavery became illegitimate as human beings were no longer regarded as legitimate objects of property and exchange. And in the communist countries, capital markets have become illegitimate, except in a very limited way, and it is no longer legitimate—or legal—to exchange private stocks and bonds.

We can roughly classify institutions and organizations in regard to the proportions of threat, exchange, and integrative elements they involve. The "social triangle" (Figure 4.1) illustrates these proportions. T shows 100 percent threat; I, 100 percent integrative structure; and E, 100 percent exchange. Any point such as H within the triangle shows HK_t, the percentage of threat; HK_i, percentage

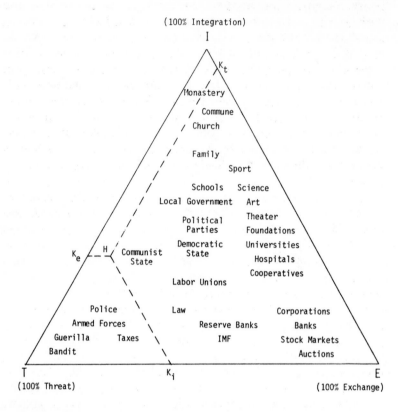

At any point H, HK_e = % Exchange, HK_i = % Integration, HK_t = % Threat.

Figure 4.1   The Social Triangle

integrative structure; and HK_e, percentage exchange. The closer to the apex T, the more threat; the closer to I, the more integrative structure; and the closer to E, the more exchange is in the mixture. Various institutions are placed in the diagram and roughly estimate the proportion of threat, integrative, and exchange structures they involve. Thus corporations, banks, stock markets, and auctions have a high proportion of exchange, not very much threat, and some integrative structure. Markets, for instance, cannot be operated without trust and a certain sense of community. Bandits, guerrillas, armed forces, and police have high proportions of threat. Armed forces and police are significantly involved with integrative structures, patriotism, and a sense of community, and also have substantial exchange relationships. Monasteries, communes, families and churches have a high proportion of integrative structure. Political institutions tend to be found somewhere in the middle, involving both legitimated threat and a fair number of exchange relationships. These proportions are very rough guesses and should not be taken for more than that.

CHAPTER *5*

The World as an Economic System

The world economy is that part of the world social system that is
organized mainly through exchange, or that involves the things
exchanged—that is, exchangeables or commodities. The prices or
exchange ratios at which things are exchanged; the production,
consumption, and stocks of commodities; the allocation of human
activity to economic matters such as the production, consumption,
and exchange of exchangeables; grants or one-way transfers of
exchangeables also come into the picture. The distributional
structure of wealth and income is also important—that is, who and
how many have assets or income of different sizes? The economy
interacts with the "polity"—that is, political structures and
institutions—in a great many ways, through taxation, subsidies,
government regulations, laws, and so on. It also interacts with the
cluster of rather vague social phenomena, which I have called the
"integry"—institutions like churches, monasteries, religious
organizations, families, clubs. Perhaps one should also include the
armed forces and war in the integrative structure, for these are a
combination of integrative and disintegrative factors and on the whole
are not governed by economic considerations.

The economic system is closely related to accounting, which is
concerned with the evaluation of complex structures and processes in
terms of a monetary unit, like the dollar. Balance sheets and income
accounts are an important feature of the economy. A balance sheet
begins with a position statement that lists all the various assets and
liabilities (negative assets) belonging to a specific organization, such
as a firm or a person. This can be done even for a nonprofit
organization, like a church or a foundation. Each of the discrete items
in the position statement, which may include such things as buildings,
machines, goods in process, stocks of finished goods, cash on hand,
debts both owed to the organization (which are assets) and owed by
the organization to others (which are liabilities), and so on, is then

transformed into a sum of monetary units—say, dollars—according to what are often fairly arbitrary rules. Items may be valued at current market prices; multiplying the quantity by the price gives us the total value. Thus if we have 1,000 barrels of oil at $30 per barrel, this amounts to a value of $30,000.

When we add the value of all the assets and liabilities together (the liabilities, of course, being negative), we get a "bottom line," which is the net worth of the organization or person concerned. This is always an approximation of the total value of the organization or person, because there are always intangibles and unmeasurables that are significant, such as the quality of the leadership, the morale of the organization, its position in various markets, the possibility of government regulation, legal suits, or the health, skills, and disposition of persons, and so on—all of which may affect measureable values in the future. These, however, have to be estimated qualitatively, and in the case of corporations they may be reflected in the market value of the stock, which may be more or less than the "book value" of the accountant, depending on the evaluation people in the market put on these intangible factors. How well the stock market evaluates these intangible factors is another matter about which there can be some dispute. The stock market seems to be guided as much by gossip, hearsay, and rumor as it is by cold accounting data and rational expectations.

A description of the economy involves a description of the production, consumption, distribution, exchange, and stocks of all commodities, together with a description of the economically relevant behavior of all persons and organizations engaged in the economy, including the image of the economy and its future they possess. It should include all changes in the political, social, or physical environment that would be relevant, and so on. This is a system of such overwhelming magnitude and complexity that nobody could possibly envisage it in all its details. We therefore have to develop simplfying concepts and classifications at the cost of losing a great deal of information about the system in order to be able to form any image of it in our minds. Sometimes the information that we throw out in this process may be significant. We always have to remember that however complex the image in our minds, it is orders of magnitude below the level of complexity of the system itself, and we should always be on the lookout for possible errors in it, especially errors of classification, in the sense that we tend to lump things together, things that should be considered separately, and much more rarely consider separately things that could be lumped together.

Because of the "measuring rod of money," it is easier to aggregate things in the economy than it is in political or other social systems. In the late nineteenth century, for instance, economists began to develop measures of the "price level" of different groups of commodities by getting some kind of weighted average measure of the change in all their money prices. These measures cannot be perfectly accurate, but as long as we recognize this fact, they can be useful. Most measures of the price level measure how much money we would have to spend in order to buy a given basketful of commodities as between one date and a later date. If on the earlier date we could buy the basketful for $100 and at a later date for $110, then we would say that the price level had risen 10 percent in the interval. Suppose, however, that we have a somewhat different basketful of commodities in different quantities and proportions on the two dates. Which basketful do we take? There is no definite answer to this question.

The problem becomes even more difficult when we have changes in the quality of commodities, which are very hard to measure, and even more when the later basketful contains new commodities altogether that did not exist in the earlier one. What, for instance, was the price of a color television set in 1930 when they did not exist? Mathematically, we might want to write this as an infinite price, multiplied by a zero quantity, which is any finite number we want to write down, but that does not do us much good. We just have to live with these unavoidable inaccuracies and recognize that any measure of the price level will somewhat exaggerate the rise in prices because of the addition of new commodities and the improvements in quality that usually take place. Sometimes, of course, there may be deterioration in quality. Commodities that existed at one time may disappear, but this is rather rare. If the price index goes, say, from 100 to 103, we cannot be quite sure that it has really gone up. If it goes from 100 to 150, we can be quite sure it has gone up. So provided that we recognize that under the apparent simplicity of a single number there is a vast complexity of different and changing commodities at different times, we will see a change in the price level index as evidence that something has happened, but something much more complex than a single number can possibly express.

The same problems arises in measures of the total output of production, consumption, investment, and so on of the economy or any section of it. Since the 1920s we have developed all over the world quite an elaborate system of national income statistics, which attempts to measure the aggregate output of the economy in terms of economic goods. The most familiar concept here is that of the gross national product. It is called "national" only because most of the calculations are done by civil servants of national states. But the concept could apply to the world as a whole (the gross world product) or any region within it (gross regional product). Theoretically, it could even be applied to nongeographical groups. We might even have a gross women's product or gross men's product or a gross Catholic product, but as far as I know, nobody has ever tried to calculate numbers like these.

The gross national product at current price levels is the total value in terms of the monetary unit of the product of the economic activity of the society, with double counting in the process of production avoided—that is, we do not count the wheat, the flour, and the bread, but only the value added as we go from wheat into flour into bread and even into toast (in restaurants, although not in households!) as we advance through the processes of production, from the rawest of raw materials to the most final of the final products. There is one exception to this: In the gross national product we do not count the depreciation of fixed capital as a negative item. When we subtract this depreciation from the gross national product, we get net national product, which, for purposes of comparison of the riches of two nations or groups, is a more significant figure.

Another figure that is frequently calculated is called the "gross (occasionally, net) domestic product," which is the gross or net national product minus production by nationals abroad, plus production by foreigners at home. This is usually a fairly small adjustment. To make things more complicated, another aggregate that is often calculated is the national income, which excludes direct taxes to government, presumably on the grounds that we get nothing for them.

One of the main purposes of these aggregates is to try to measure whether a nation, a region, or a group is getting richer or poorer. This reflects the fact that underneath all the enormous complexity of the economic system there is a great simplicity, an order of riches and poverty. We all know poverty when we see it—poor housing, poor clothes, a poor diet, poor health, confinement to a very small area, poor education, illiteracy, sometimes backbreaking work for long hours, sometimes no work at all, boring and corrupting idleness in the midst of squalor. By contrast, we have a middle group that can at least have good housing, good food, good health, good education, enough leisure for recreation, travel, culture, the arts, sports, political activity, and so on. At the far end of the scale we have the very rich who live in palaces, have many homes in elegant places, jet around the world, and are virtually unlimited in their activities by any consideration of expenses or any question of being able to afford things. One is reminded of the famous remark attributed to Mr. J. P. Morgan, the richest man in the world at the time. When someone asked him how much it cost to run a yacht, he replied, "If you have to ask that question, you can't afford it."

We also have a strong impression that some countries and regions are richer than others. There are poor countries in which a large proportion of the population suffers from poverty, although some may be rich. There are middle-income countries in which there may still be considerable numbers of poor people, but in which also a considerable part of the population lives in middle-income comfort. Then there are rich countries, which have a small proportion, or virtually no people, in real poverty and a large proportion of the population lives in comfort, with perhaps a small proportion at the top in affluence. Economic aggregates are an attempt to get more accurate measures of these impressions.

There are many difficulties involved, however. One that has been much neglected is the relative role of stocks of economic goods in relation to the additions to and subtractions from these stocks, which is income. The confusion between stocks and flows—that is, additions to and subtractions from stocks—has plagued economics almost from its beginning. It has been an unexamined assumption that riches and poverty relate only to income—that is, to production (the addition to stocks) and consumption (the subtraction from stocks). Most satisfaction, however, comes from the use of goods rather than from their consumption. I get no satisfaction out of the fact that my clothes, my house, my furniture, my car, and even my body are wearing out. I get satisfaction from wearing clothes, living in a house, driving my car, and having my body well fed and in good health. On the other hand, I do take some satisfaction in buying a new suit and getting a new book, and I certainly get satisfaction out of eating as well as being well fed. I get satisfaction, also, out of the act of production—painting a picture, writing a book, teaching a class, doing something that other people value, and so on.

It is very hard to put these things together into a single figure. Nevertheless, as we have seen earlier, in any system stocks and flows are closely related. The increase in a stock or population is always equal to the additions minus the subtractions. In this case, additions are production and subtractions are consumption in the literal sense of the term. There is some confusion of terms here because economists have often used "consumption" to mean household purchases, that commodities simply disappeared once they were purchased by a householder. This is unrealistic, as household capital now is probably larger than industrial capital. Wealth, however, is a stock; income is the flow through it, whether production or consumption. It is clear that we cannot increase our wealth if our income is so small that we consume it all. This is one of the great problems of the persistence of poverty. There is a level of income below which it is virtually impossible to increase wealth. Indeed, when income falls below this level, consumption almost has to exceed income, simply in order for people to stay alive. When wealth diminishes and becomes negative, we get debt. At a certain level of income, therefore, we tend to get stable poverty. In order to get richer, we have to accumulate something, whether this is knowledge and skill, tools and equipment, or bodily health and strength that comes from adequate nutrition and healthful environments. This may mean diminishing "bads," such as getting rid of rats, mosquitos, and sewage, as well as increasing goods. When income is low enough there is nothing available for accumulation and enrichment. At still lower levels of income poverty increases, and people slide down into destitution, hunger, famine, and utter misery, from which they cannot escape without outside help unless population reduction increases the per capita resources of the survivors.

The problem of the instability of inequality is also part of the picture of the economy, although it also applies to other parts of the social system. This derives from what has been called the "Matthew Principle," because it is cited three times in the Gospel of St. Matthew in the New Testament—that "to him that hath shall be given, and to him that hath not shall be taken away, even that which he hath" (13:12, 25, 29). Suppose we started off with a system of absolutely equal income and wealth. Random fluctuations would make some people a little richer than others. The richer would find it easier to get still richer because it would be easier to keep consumption down below income. The poorer would find it harder to get richer and easier to get poorer, as it would become harder to get income above consumption and inequality would begin to develop. It would be checked, however, by a complex set of factors. At some point, the richer would start to lose their riches with bad investments or inheritance by spendthrifts. Any increase in the general level of riches of a society does tend to trickle down to the poor, and society also develops a "grants economy"—that is, one-way transfers—to the poor from the richer through taxation, public expenditures, and grants. So at some point the movement toward inequality is checked. Something like at least a temporary equilibrium comes into being. We see this in the United States, where the proportional distribution of income has changed very little in the last 40 years or so in spite of the New Deal, progressive taxation, the "war against poverty," and even a bit of "war against the poor" in the 1980s.

Economic development is the process of getting richer. This is a complex process involving a good deal of positive feedback. It is a process that can be halted or even reversed, particularly by adverse political systems—as we have seen, for instance, in Argentina and Uruguay. It can be halted also by population expansion, as we see now in some African countries. If a country doubles its population in a single generation, as some of these countries are doing, this means that just to stay where they are requires a doubling of the housing, the equipment, the whole capital stock of the society, and this may not be easy, especially as in the early stages of population increase there will be large numbers of children and young people who are not much in the labor force, so the proportion of population in the labor force will decline. This also makes it much harder to educate the children, and as the human learning process is the key to economic development, this may be the greatest handicap.

Nevertheless, economic development has taken place over a considerable part of the world, especially in about the last 300 years, and may well have accelerated in the twentieth century in spite of the world wars, the Great Depression, and the division of the world into centrally planned and market economies. Economic development often begins with an improvement in the productivity of agriculture. This can lead to better nutrition and a healthier and more active labor force, and it may release workers from agriculture to do other things—for instance, manufacturing and construction. We see this dramatically in the United States, where the proportion of the labor force in agriculture has gone from about 80 percent in 1776 to 22 percent in 1929 to less than 4 percent today, although we should probably add to that the labor engaged in producing agricultural machinery and other facilitating factors. This has certainly released some 15 percent of the labor force, who have gone into other occupations, especially into government, education, the service trades, and so on. Manufacturing has been rather stable, as improvements in manufacturing have also liberated some of the labor force to go into these other occupations, as well as, in intervening periods, into unemployment, a problem we will discuss later.

A similar phenomenon was observable in Britain in the first half of the eighteenth century with the enclosure movement, which created farms rather than the scattered strips of the medieval village. Farms were then capable of improvement and the substitution of the medieval fallow field by root crops, especially turnips and clover, tremendously increased the yield, especially of animal fodder, per farm acre and led to an extraordinary improvement in livestock in both size and productivity. This improved the quantity and the quality of the human food supply, increasing protein intake. This seems to have led to a remarkable diminution in infant mortality in the middle of the eighteenth century, and, of course, a population explosion. The labor, including the children, released from agriculture found their way into other occupations, such as the rising manufacturing sector, to some extent, no doubt, into building elegant country houses for the landlords, but also into investment in increasing productivity in other areas. Even with all the dislocations and human suffering involved in all this, there is no doubt that the end result was a much richer society.

There are three major factors in getting richer. One is an increase in the productivity of human activity, with more and more valuable goods produced per hour, essentially by human time-saving. Another is increase in productivity per acre or unit of land, land-saving either by increasing yields of crops or by building skyscrapers. Increase in productivity virtually always involves human learning, finding out new ways of doing things. Usually it also involves an increase in the energy input into the processes of production. From the eighteenth century on this has come mainly from the use of fossil fuels—first coal, later oil and gas, now to a much smaller extent uranium 235.

Production, whether of a biological organism, a fertilized egg, or a human artifact like a suit of clothes, a house, a chair, or an automobile (which constitute riches), always originates in some genetic factor, which could be called "know-how." There were no steam engines before about 1710 and no automobiles before about 1880, for one very good reason: We did not know how to make them. Exactly the same reason accounts for the fact that there were no human beings ten million years ago. The genetic structure of the earth did not know how to make us. Know-how, however, is not enough. There must also be an adequate supply of the "limiting factors." The genetic structure has to be able to capture energy in order to transport and transform selected materials into the form of the product, whether this is the chicken from the egg or the automobile from blueprints and the know-how embodied in the minds of the automobile industry and its feeders. Without energy and materials—and, we should add, space and time—all the know-how in the world will not produce anything. One thing that is often overlooked in the case of the limiting factors is that it is the *most* limiting one that limits production. Thus in the production of biological organisms this may be energy, as it certainly is at the poles, or it may be some material, like water, in the Sahara, or the absence of soil, and so on. Similarly, in economic production the limits may be set by the scarcity of land in an overpopulated area, by a deficiency of energy or fuel, as perhaps in the case of the Eskimos or the tribes of the tropical forest.

With the enormous rise in human knowledge and know-how in the last 200 or 300 years, however, natural resources such as land, mines, oil wells, and water became less and less important as a source of riches and in explaining the distribution of riches around the world, and human knowledge and know-how became overwhelmingly important. This is mainly the result of the development of the system of world trade involving exchange and the transport of commodities of all kinds, including natural resources, and products all around the world. Water transportation is still very important in this process, as it is still much cheaper for moving bulk materials than is land transportation, although it takes more time. Transportation by air takes less time but is very expensive. It increasingly pays off, however, when time-saving is important, as with perishable foods.

Trade, of course, involves know-how just as much as manufacturing or agriculture does. People have to know where things are, how to get there, and who has to be negotiated with. There has to be know-what, know-where, and know-whom. All this has to be learned. The recipe for getting rich is to develop both skill in production and skill at trade. This seems to be a major limiting factor. Japan has been getting richer at an unprecedented rate in the last few decades, tailing off a bit now, mainly because Japan is a remarkable learning society, and the obstacles to human learning seem much less than they are in many other societies. Japan has very little in the way of natural resources, but this has not been an important limiting factor. Japan has been able to buy natural resources and energy from all over the world in exchange for the products Japanese skill and ingenuity have made with the aid of these natural resources. Resource-rich countries may even be impoverished by their very resources if they divert attention from the fundamental learning processes that are the only long-run sources of enrichment.

It was Adam Smith who first recognized that exchange, the relative price structure that results from it, the division of labor and specialization of production it encourages, is what we would call today a "positive feedback" process that leads into enrichment of the whole—although some, of course, may get richer faster than others. This is in his famous Chapter 3 (Book I) of *The Wealth of Nations,* that the "division of labour" is limited by the "extent of the market." The division of labor and specialization encourage a learning process that increases productivity, which increases the products to be exchanged, which increases exchange, which in turn permits greater specialization, greater productivity, greater exchange, and so on. This process involves not only the learning of manual skills but also the development of a specialized class of what Adam Smith calls "philosophers" (what we would call scientists and engineers), who specialize in the increase of knowledge and its application to production.

The great expansion and unification of the world economy began around 1860 with the application of science to the production of goods, starting off with the chemical industry, beginning with aniline dyes and going on to an enormous range of substances unknown to the world before. Then the 1880s began the electrical industry, which produced an enormous transformation of human comfort and productivity, both in the home and in the workplace, because of the remarkable subdividability of electrical energy, seen today perhaps in the extreme form in small solar-powered calculators. Electrical energy involves an energy cost, in the sense that the energy that comes out of the wire or the laser beam is less than what went into the power station. But this is more than compensated for by an enormous increase in convenience and utilization.

In the twentieth century the biological sciences have produced an enormous increase in agricultural productivity, with such innovations as hybrid corn, and now an enormous potential is opening up for genetic engineering. This has enabled world food production to keep up roughly with the population explosion, although there are now signs that this is no longer happening, especially in Africa.

The development of the steel industry and metallurgy also owes a great deal to the application of science, which helped to give us skyscrapers and steamships in the nineteenth century; the internal combustion engine and the jet airplane enormously expanded the capacity of the human race for travel and for transporting things. Again, this contributed to the expansion of world trade. Sea transport has been transformed by the so-called container revolution of the last two or three decades, which has greatly improved the process of getting things from ship to land, and vice versa. Pipelines have greatly diminished the cost of transporting gas, oil, and even potentially coal through a coal slurry.

This whole developmental process is essentially an evolutionary system with many parallels to biological evolution, with mutation in the form of human learning, new knowledge and know-how, invention, and discovery. The filling of an empty niche by one successful mutation has then created large numbers of empty niches elsewhere to be filled by other mutations. In the course of this development the world has become increasingly a single economic system, even though, like the biosphere, it still consists of many subsystems that have a pattern, processes, and degree of independence of their own. A thousand years ago, of course, there was no world economy any more than there was a single world social system. The world was divided into large numbers of economies with very little contact with each other. The American continents had no contact whatever with the Old World. Even within the American continents, the Aztecs, as far as we know, had no contact with the Incas. Europe had virtually no contact with Asia or with Africa below the Sahara.

It was a few rather slow improvements in ocean transportation and in navigation that opened up the world as a single unit for the human race. The development of the rudder, whereby ships could be steered on an accurate course, and improvements in sails seem to have been the key factors. This may have begun with the Ming voyages from China to Africa in the early fifteenth century. Then came Vasco da Gama and the rounding of the Cape, partly the result of the Turkish capture of Constantinople cutting off trade from the Mediterranean eastward. It is ironic how the military victory of the Turks seems to have led to their economic and scientific stagnation, and by response almost to the enormous expansion of Europe all over the world. Then, of course, came Columbus. Some unkind person once said, "How could Columbus miss it, if you could go 3,000 miles in a straight line?" Then came the expansion of Europe into the Americas, and also into China and Japan by way of the Jesuits. Marco Polo had pioneered this earlier and went to China. Trade followed the flag and mostly the flag followed trade, with the expansion of the British Empire in India, the Dutch in Indonesia, and so on. Both the United States and Russia expanded over land to the Pacific in the nineteenth century. Since the end of World War II we have seen an extraordinary explosion in world trade, surprisingly little recognized, with the total volume increasing some six times.

Economically, however, there are still two worlds rather than one, even though within each of these two worlds there are enormous differences. There is the communist world composed of Russia, the Eastern European countries, China, Vietnam, Cuba, and—somewhat unwillingly—Afghanistan and North Korea; and the capitalist world, which is the rest of it. This is, of course, a great oversimplification. Within the communist world we have enormous differences and great internal hostilities. Yugoslavia has always been an exception and is a sort of "halfway house" between communism and capitalism. China and Russia exhibit a good deal more enmity than there is between Russia and the United States. And China has made a substantial turn toward market economies, although it has by no means given up the principle of central planning. China is even having a sporadic war with Vietnam, which is a Russian protege. Hungary has become a considerably freer society than it was ten or fifteen years ago. Poland has had the great uprising of Solidarity. While this has been suppressed, Poland will never be quite the same again.

Within the capitalist world there are even wider differences. One is tempted to say there is no such thing as capitalism. It is a name for an enormous diversity of systems. It changes all the time in a constant process of evolution. We certainly cannot say when capitalism began. We can do a little better at putting a beginning date on communism: the Russian Revolution of 1917. Some of the institutions of capitalism, however, go back a long way into ancient civilizations. Property and trade, money, banking, bills of exchange, foreign exchanges, businesses—these all have antecedents in the ancient world. The Roman Empire was certainly not a centrally planned economy, even though it had a large public sector. Feudalism in a sense represented something of a retreat from a market economy, with serfdom and status obligations, and a great deal of barter and exchange in kind, but the feudal system certainly never abandoned money, and trade went on at fairs and even internationally.

The invention of double-entry bookkeeping and more accurate accounting goes back to twelfth- and thirteenth-century Italy. It is something of a landmark, with the provision of a more accurate measure of profit. Debt is certainly an ancient institution. Partnerships are equally ancient. The corporation and the institution of stockholders is a little more modern. Organized stock exchanges go back to the sixteenth century in Europe. Limited liability is an invention of the nineteenth century, but the multinational corporation certainly goes back to the East India Company, although it has become much more important in the twentieth century. Nevertheless, today there is a sharp distinction between the centrally planned and the market economies. Private ownership of the means of production is prohibited in centrally planned economies on a large scale and is barely tolerated on a small scale. Profit is a much less significant element of the system in centrally planned economies, although in its looser forms, as in Yugoslavia and now in China, it is by no means unknown. But it does not have the vital significance that it has in market societies.

There are critical questions about the long-run stability of both market societies and centrally planned economies. Well-run market economies are favorable to economic development. The historical evidence suggests that as these countries get richer the proportion of national income going to labor increases, although it seems difficult to get much proportional change in the distribution of income. The amount of poverty continually decreases, simply because everybody gets richer. In the United States, for instance, the amount of poverty by any standard was halved between 1947 and about 1970, but this happened not through redistribution but simply because everybody got twice as rich. If the poor get twice as rich, this halves the amount of poverty. At the same time the middle class got twice as rich and so did the rich, so that there was not much redistribution or change in the proportional shares of the various groups.

The gravest weakness, and perhaps ultimately the Achilles heel, of the market economies is unemployment and the tendency for falling into depressions. This, again, is a complex phenomenon which I think we understand much much better than we did 50 or 60 years ago, largely thanks to John Maynard Keynes and some others and to the development of national income statistics, which at least has enabled us to test ideas that previously were untestable. I remember Professor Schumpeter once saying, "How nice economics was before anybody knew anything"—perhaps because then one could spin theories without having to test them! As a rough approximation, one can say that in market economies unemployment occurs when it does not pay employers to employ as many people as there are in the labor force in the private sector, and the government does not increase its employment sufficiently to take up the slack.

The greatest crisis of capitalism was unquestionably the Great Depression of the 1930s, when unemployment in the United States went to 25 percent of the labor force in 1932 and 1933, and was even a greater percentage in some countries like Australia and Germany. If we ask why this 25 percent of the labor force was not employed, we have to ask, why do employers employ people? Some people may be employed by households as servants, painters, or gardeners, but this is a small proportion. Certainly in developed societies most wage workers are employed by businesses. If we ask why a business employs people, the answer is that it pays to employ them if the profit resulting from the product of the work is greater than the interest that would be received if the money spent on the wage were put out as a loan.

Just how profit is earned on the work is a complex matter. From the point of view of the cost accountant, the money spent on the wage is reflected in the value added to the real capital of the business. This may take the form of lessening the depreciation of the fixed capital (maintenance, repairs, and so on), or it may take the form of transforming goods in process into more finished goods of higher value. The process of production involves the transformation of materials or goods that are taken into the firm into goods that are eventually sold out of the firm. If a laborer, for instance, grinds wheat into flour, the value of the flour, according to the cost accountant, is equal to the amount spent on wages, which is a deduction from the money stock of the firm, plus the value of the supplies used up, which is a deduction from the flour stock, plus any depreciation on machinery or buildings used in the process. If, then, the final product is sold for more than it cost, there is a profit.

In cost accounting the total net worth of the firm does not change. Some items in the balance sheet go up and some other items go down in equal amounts. When the product is sold for more than its cost, then the net worth goes up and there is profit. If this profit is greater than the rise in net worth that would result from putting the money spent on the wage out to interest, then it pays to employ the laborer; otherwise, it does not. Beyond a certain point, the more laborers are employed, the less will be the profit, as the actual product may have to be sold at reduced prices unless there is absolutely perfect competition, which is rare. The firm, then, will stop increasing its employment at the point where the sacrifice of the wage is estimated not to cover the gain in profit. This, of course, is always something of a rough estimate. We can never be sure what profit is going to be, and these estimates may change with waves of optimism and pessimism, and so on.

Another factor in the decision to employ people may be the relative proportions of different items in the firm's position statement. Suppose, for instance, there is a large accumulation of unsold final product and, as a result, the money stock of the firm is very low. Under these circumstances, hiring somebody will run down the money stock still further and will increase unwanted inventories. Hence the firm will have to be very optimistic that the unwanted inventories will be sold and the money stock replenished, or else the worker will not be hired.

If we look at the situation in the United States in 1932 and 1933 (and it was not very different in the rest of the capitalist world), we find that real rates of interest were still on the order of 3 percent and profit rates were actually negative. Under these circumstances, it is almost literally true that anybody who hired anybody was either a philanthropist, a fool, or a creature of habit, for whoever hired anybody was bound to lose by it and could have done much better by putting money out to interest. In fact, one wonders why the unemployment rate did not go to 50 or 75 percent and the whole society break down under these circumstances. The answer can only be that businesses kept going out of habit or because they put a high value on keeping the organization together. The accumulation of unwanted inventories during these years was also a significant factor, as was a virtual cessation of construction and investments in fixed capital. Net investments in these years, indeed, were negative. The capital stock was diminishing and not being replaced because there was no profit in replacing it and maintaining it. This happened, furthermore, under governments that were friendly to market economies and wanted to preserve them.

An understanding of exactly how this happened is of great importance in estimating the future of capitalism, for we certainly cannot avoid a possible repetition of situations of this kind unless we understand them and know what to do about them. Herbert Hoover did not understand what was happening and had no idea what to do about it. Franklin Roosevelt was about equally ignorant, but he did cheer people up. Investment started again and profits revived, and we began to climb out of the Great Depression. It was almost as if we went to a cliff and did not fall off it but backed away from it. Coming to such a cliff in the future and going over it is a haunting prospect.

The remedy of the Classical and neo-Classical economists for unemployment was a reduction in money wages. Keynes's great insight showed that this might not solve the problem, simply because a general reduction in money wages would diminish the demand for finished products. This would either lead to a further piling up of inventories, which would discourage employment, or, if prices were cut, this would diminish profits, and real wages would not change much. There would probably be some kind of a limit to this process, but it could easily be at a level of unemployment that is quite unacceptable. At some point the decline in production might be sufficient so that inventories would decline and investment, profits, and employment would revive. This could easily be at high levels of unemployment. The Keynesian solution, which ironically is being applied by President Reagan today, is to run a sufficient cash deficit in the government budget so that money stocks in the hands of the public will increase, household purchases will increase, inventories will diminish, opportunities for fixed investment will possibly be found, and unemployment will decline.

We would put the whole matter in a slightly different way by pointing to a very obvious truism—that everything produced by businesses in a given period has either been purchased by households or by government or is still in the hands of businesses in the form of investment (additions to capital). In order to sustain full employment, the full employment product must be divided between what is taken off the hands of businesses by households and government, leaving an increase in the products in the hands of business, which businesses are willing to accept as investment. If they are not willing to accept this increase, they will cut back on production and employment in an attempt to reduce stocks of goods; this will reduce household purchases out of reduced incomes; and so the stocks and goods in the hands of business will be reduced much less than the decline in production. If they are still considered to be excessive, the decline in production and employment will go on, until we get to a level low enough that unwanted goods are no longer accumulating in the hands of business. This could easily be at a disastrously low level.

Market economies are also subject to certain other pathologies. Organized competitive markets—like the wheat or cotton market or the stock market—tend to exhibit rather meaningless fluctuations in the general level of their prices because of speculative movements, again with a kind of positive feedback effect. If prices are perceived by the people in the market as being low, there will be a rush to buy and prices will rise, confirming the belief that they were going to rise. If people think they will rise still further, they will continue to buy, so prices do rise still further. This goes on until prices are perceived to be high, after which the expectation that they will fall begins to grow, more people want to sell than to buy, prices then do fall, this confirms the expectation, and the fall continues. Prices go on falling until they become low again, after which the process starts again. These fluctuations can be quite irregular, but they can be very disturbing to the economy. It was the collapse of the stock market in 1929, for instance, that set off the processes that led to the Great Depression.

Another pathology of market economies is inflation, which has been almost universal in the last three decades. This is mainly a result of government policy, especially of government deficits, particularly cash deficits in which the government pays out more cash than it takes in from taxes. This creates more money in the hands of the public. If the government takes in $100 million and pays out $110 million, obviously there is $10 million more in the hands of the public. Budget deficits, of course, can be financed by borrowing as well as by the creation of new money, and this, again, has complex and sometimes quite adverse effects; for instance, in raising interest rates.

A moderate rate of inflation does not seem to disturb market economies very much. In fact, it operates as a kind of tax on idle money. The cash I hold in my sock will be worth less next year if all prices have risen. On the other hand, there is some tendency, particularly with irresponsible governments, for inflation to accelerate and some danger that this will lead to hyperinflation, the sort of thing that happened in Germany in 1923 and in Hungary in 1946, when the price level sometimes doubled every week or more, when people dashed from the pay window to the store, knowing that prices would have doubled in a day or two. This is an intolerable situation, which may lead to the very destruction of capitalism, as it did in Hungary, and also to the destruction of democracy, as it eventually did in Germany. It has always been followed, however, by some kind of stabilization.

Centrally planned economies suffer from a set of diseases different from those that afflict capitalism, but they are sometimes even more severe. Just as the kind of rigorous laissez-faire ideology that has sometimes dominated the governments of capitalist societies is a great handicap when it comes to a realistic appraisal of how market societies need to be governed, a rigid Marxist or Marxist-Leninist ideology is a great handicap in the development of centrally planned economies toward both riches and personal freedoms. Marxism is to be taken seriously. Marx had some profound insights. If we think of Marxism as one step down the road toward a realistic and accurate image of society, as indeed Ptolemy was an important step down the road toward the accurate image of the solar system that we have today, it would be much more fruitful than if we regard Marx as revealed truth not to be altered.

The great unsolved problem of centrally planned economies is the inevitable concentration of both political and economic power they imply. In democratic, social-capitalist societies political power is, at least in part, separated from economic power, and there are checks and balances that deter extreme concentrations of power and force them into compromise and tolerance. When power is as concentrated as it is in centrally planned economies, there is always a probability that it will be seized by someone who does not really have the skill to exercise it wisely. There is no political apparatus, except death, for the removal from power of incompetent, ignorant, or even pathologically malevolent personalities. Oddly enough, Stalin's First

Collectivization was a greater disaster for the Soviet Union than was the Great Depression at the same time in the capitalist world. At least five million people lost their lives, and among these the ablest farmers in Soviet agriculture. Collectivized agriculture and state farms are notoriously inefficient. Indeed, if had it not been for the vestigial private plots, the Soviet situation would have been much worse in terms of actual starvation. Soviet agriculture has never recovered from Stalin. It still has some 30 to 35 percent of the labor force, which is the way American agriculture was in 1900. This inability to transfer labor out of agriculture accounts, at least in part, for the poor housing, poor consumer goods, and rather drab lives of the mass of the Soviet people.

China is another example where a brilliant, charismatic leader who unified the country, Mao Tse Tung, in his later life made catastrophic mistakes of policy. For instance, the "Great Leap Forward" turned out to be a great leap sideways if not, in fact, even backwards. The Cultural Revolution, while in some ways well intentioned, was catastrophic for the educational, scientific, and cultural community and left a scar that will take many years to heal.

The greatest catastrophe of all is Cambodia (Kampuchea) under Pol Pot. It is estimated that between half a million and two million people were killed out of a population of six million. Those killed included virtually all of the ablest and best educated, and the whole country has been reduced to near starvation and utter poverty. It is the most appalling example of the utter destructiveness of class war that nobody—least of all the poor—could possibly win. Vietnam, again, seems to be a society of endless misery, oppression, and war.

On the other end of the scale we have Yugoslavia and Hungary, which are at least fairly cheerful and relaxed centrally planned economies with a good deal of personal freedom and at least modest economic success. East Germany has had some economic success, largely because it is German in culture, but at a very high cost in the drabness and the oppressiveness of the society. In Poland, the incompetence of the communist leadership produced a popular uprising in the form of Solidarity. Bulgaria seems to be a more cheerful and successful society than Rumania. Czechoslovakia is perhaps the saddest of all the communist countries, where the centrally planned economy is clearly maintained only by the oppressive power of threat. Cuba is also a society with a rigid centrally planned economy. It has made substantial achievements in education and bringing the poorest portion of the population more into the life of the society, but it has accomplished this only at an appalling human cost in terms of the loss of its ablest and most active people, most of whom have immigrated to the United States and, again, in terms of the drabness of daily life and forced hypocritical conformity to established doctrines.

Perhaps the saddest countries of all are those that have fallen apart through internal conflict, like Lebanon and El Salvador, or those that have tried to resolve internal conflict by repressive and inhumane regimes, mainly military, like Argentina and Uruguay. In general, the military have made poor rulers from the point of view of a successful economy, perhaps because war is a profoundly uneconomic enterprise and the military ideology stresses absolute values, like victory, rather than the relative values and the careful balancing of gain by loss that is characteristic of economic behavior and economic organization. Military power is essentially a negative-sum process in which what one party gains is always less than what the other party loses. Economic power, by contrast, is a positive-sum process in which, typically, everybody gains, and even when some lose, those who gain gain much more than those who lose lose. It is not surprising, therefore, that military government, or even militaristic government, tends toward economic failure. In comparison with Argentina, Australia over the last 40 years illustrates the point. These countries are similar in terms of geography, European migration and mobilization, railroad development, wheat and cattle exports, and so on, and they had about the same per capita income in the 1930s. From about 1945 on, however, Argentina stagnated economically as Australia got richer at a modest but steady pace, and today Australia has close to three times the per capita income of Argentina after about two generations. The impact of politics in economic life can hardly be demonstrated more dramatically. It is clear that the world as an economic system is closely related to the world as a political system, and we will look at that in the next chapter.

CHAPTER 6

The World as a Political System

All important distinctions are a little fuzzy, and it is by no means easy to say where the economic system ends and the political system begins. Nevertheless, there is a rough approximate division. We might say that the economic system, or the economy, consists of those aspects of the social system that are organized primarily through legitimated exchange (even occasionally illegitimate exchange, like drug trafficking or the white slave trade, as it used to be called), whereas the political system consists of those forms of social organization that depend primarily on legitimated threat. Again, the line between what is legitimate and illegitimate is not wholly clear. A guerrilla band might be regarded as illegitimate by its victims but highly legitimate by the band itself. If the guerrillas ever succeed in establishing a legitimate government, they cease to be called terrorists and become merely an armed force.

Another concept that is very important in political systems is that of leadership and hierarchy. This, too, is a complex phenomenon and always involves some kind of legitimacy and hence is deeply involved with integrative structures. In Chester Barnard's classic work on organization theory, *The Functions of the Executive* (1938), it is observed that authority is always granted from below in the hierarchy, and unless it is so granted, it is very insecure. Authority, or leadership, rests on a variety of social relationships, partly on threat; partly on integrative relationships such as charisma and the capacity to command assent to leadership, which may be the most important. There may also be hidden economic factors in it, particularly in what is called the "grants economy." The leader may have goods to bestow in return for services and the approval of the followers. In formal organizations, however, the threat system is also very important. The leader can threaten the follower with expulsion or punishment. The relation of a common soldier to an officer or a general, even of a clergyman to the head of his church, a teacher to the school superintendent, a worker to his boss, has elements of a threat in it. It may simply be what is called "discipline"—that is, nasty things will happen to you if you don't follow instructions. Or it may be the threat of being expelled from an organization—that is, a worker might be fired, a soldier court-martialed, a priest unfrocked, a professor dismissed, and so on. Such threats underlie a great many organizational and political relationships, especially in more extreme positions of the system.

A striking case of the use of legitimated threat in political systems is the whole structure of the law, including particularly taxes. We pay our taxes mainly because if we did not we would get into more trouble than we think it would be worth. We can easily estimate how much of our tax payment is due to threat if we ask ourselves how much would we pay the government in taxes if it was financed by a United Fund or voluntary contributions. The difference, which is usually substantial, is due to threat. The apparatus of criminal law is an example of an attempt at deterrence by no means wholly effective, although it is always argued that crime would be much higher if there were no deterrence. Threat is thus very much a part of the political system. When we look for the political structures of society, we find them mainly in law and war.

The early history of political systems is obscure. They seem to have an almost universal tendency to originate in kin groups and the extended family. Even the nuclear family of parents and children has political aspects and it seems to be difficult to raise children without a certain amount of threat, and the status of parents to children is certainly one of hierarchy. The almost universal existence of rites of passage from childhood into adulthood in human societies suggests that a child is not a full political being. The relation of the parent to the child in most cultures has some similarities to that of the slave-owner and the slave, although there are also important differences, in the sense that the parent has an interest in the child's eventual "emancipation" into adulthood.

There is also a strong reciprocity principle at work in the family that has not been wholly destroyed even by Social Security and the welfare state. Parents support children through childhood in the understanding that the children will support their parents in their old age. This is one of the most universal of cultural traits, even in diverse cultures. One of the Ten Commandments, "Honor your father and your mother that your days may be long in the land which the Lord your God gives you," is a striking example (Exodus 20:12). If we honor our father and our mother, then our children will honor us as their father and mother. In the extended family or kinship group, there is a strong tendency for leadership to be established by age because age dependency is so important in the history of the family. The traditional Chinese family is supposed to be one of the prime examples of this.

It has been argued by Sir Henry Maine and Lewis Morgan in the later nineteenth century that a fundamental transition in political terms is that of the transition from the kin-based group to the domicile or habitat-based group. Some of this depends on the nature of human migration and settlements. In the case of hunting-gathering societies there is a strong tendency for the political group to be a kin group, and if in the course of population increase this group splits off a segment that goes somewhere else and starts another group, these will be the founding parents who create another kin group. With agriculture the groups became much larger, so there had to be admission of nonkin into the group, although the history of this is obscure. Genealogy is certainly one of the earliest forms of history in an oral form. We see it reflected, for instance, in the genealogies in the Bible. The Jews thought of themselves as the descendants of Abraham, with a sharp separation genealogically between themselves and the Gentiles.

The expansion of Christianity had something to do with the fact that even the early church was a nonkin group, thanks, perhaps, to St. Paul, and nonkin groups have the potential for expanding more rapidly than the kin group. The early Christian church, however, was simply following the example of the Roman Empire, which admitted all sorts of people to Roman citizenship, like St. Paul himself, who were by no means descended from Romulus and Remus. This transition from the kin group to the nonkin group was manifested in the rise even of the earliest empires. This clearly involved some kind of charismatic legitimation of the nonkin leader. Why this took so long in the history of the human race is a very interesting question. The extraordinary stability of paleolithic societies has always puzzled me. They consisted of human beings who were genetically virtually identical with those of the modern day, who possessed the same urge for curiosity and the capacity for language but who changed their basic culture very little over 40,000 years. This phenomenon may have something to do with the difficulty of the transition from the kin group to the nonkin group.

The rise of empire after Sargon and the development of cities (civilization) made political structures less dependent on kin, even though kin groups have never quite disappeared from politics, as we see in the hereditary monarchies or even in the Duponts, the Adamses, and the Kennedys in the United States. How far the development of agriculture permitted the rise of nonkin groups, or whether it was the rise of nonkin groups that developed agriculture, I think we really do not know. It is clear that there is a close relationship here between agriculture and civilization. I think it is true to say that no preagricultural society ever really developed cities or empires. This is perhaps because while hunting-gathering societies sometimes had food surpluses in favorable environments, these were not usually very storable. Both the grains on which Old World agriculture depended and the potatoes and corn of the New World were storable and transportable. This opened up a niche of opportunity for organized threat systems in the shape of political structures with soldiers who could take away the farmers' surpluses and transport and store them in the cities, from which stores the ruler could then feed the soldiers, and, of course, the architects, the builders, the scribes, and the artisans who constituted the cities. As noted earlier, the earliest civilizations seem to have been the priesthoods using a transcendental type of threat. These were nearly always replaced by kings who used a more physical threat.

A critical question here is the processes by which powerful political roles come to be occupied. The use of organized threat in war has certainly been an important element here. On the other hand, legitimation has also been an important element. An incompetent ruler might command armies, but he was quite likely to be overthrown either by one of his subordinates or by an invading army. There is a difference here between the use of war as a destroyer of cities and civilizations, as we saw in the case of the Mongols (Genghis Khan, Tamerlane, and so on) and war as a means of simply getting the conquerors into the old powerful roles, as nearly always seemed to have happened in China. The exercise of threat by war always requires loyalty and acceptance of leadership by those who carry out the orders of the leader. This always involves creating an image of competence and power that is acceptable to the followers. Hitler could not have risen to power, for instance, if he had not had charismatic powers of persuasion to convince his followers, at least in the early stages, that he was indeed a leader who could carry out their wishes. The fact that charisma is often little related to reality is a major creator of human tragedy and misery.

The cost of replacing an old incapable leader with a new one, whether the old one is discredited or merely dies, can sometimes be extremely high for the participants in the conflict. It is not surprising that ritualistic modes of avoiding such conflicts come into being very early. One of these, of course, is the institution of hereditary succession into powerful roles, as we see it in the hereditary monarchy. Thomas Schelling (1960) referred to this as the principle of the "salient solution." If there is one choice among many that is salient, in the sense that it stands out and no other alternative possesses this property, this makes a resolution of conflict much easier. This is why, for instance, so many bargains over prices or wages end by "splitting the difference" between the bargainers. The king's son (or, if he had no son, even the daughter) was the salient solution to the problem of who would next occupy the royal role, and it was surprisingly common in human history, even going down to the next of kin when the ruler had no direct descendants, like James I of England, or sometimes going to a more distant relation if the next of kin was unacceptable, as in the case of the English Stuarts and the selection of William and Mary as monarchs in 1688.

The hereditary principle, however, has some serious defects. A good king often had an incompetent son. In fact, this was common, simply because growing up under the shadow of a great father was likely to create several personal maladjustments and political incompetence, although there were exceptions to this rule. As society became more complicated, the hereditary principle eventually was abandoned in most societies, simply because there was too great a risk of producing incompetence in positions of power. We then got the development of other rituals, like elections and the various forms of democracy. The origins of these processes can be traced to ancient Greece, especially Athens. These, however, were very small societies and democracy was not regarded as more than a transient phase, especially by Plato. Plato distinguished five types of government or political structures (these are more or less in order of descending competence): aristocracy, which means the rule of the best; timocracy, the rule of a benign military; oligarchy, the rule of a few; the closed group, not necessarily the best, usually involving plutocracy, the rule of the rich—again, according to Plato, not necessarily the best; democracy (for Plato, it was pretty much the rule of the mob, or, at best, the inexpert); and tyranny, the rule of a single evil tyrant through naked threats to produce conformity at all costs. Certainly combinations of these have appeared at various times and places in history.

Aristocracy, of course, sounds delightful, but unfortunately nobody has ever devised a pattern of achieving power that would ensure that only those best able to exercise it would occupy the powerful roles. If one wants to be pessimistic, indeed, one can invoke what I have elsewhere called the "dismal theorem of political science"—that all the skills leading to the rise to power tend to unfit people to exercise it. While there are some exceptions to this principle, there are a deplorable number of good examples of it. A person rises to power by pushing the other contenders down, in some cases by murder, frequently by deceit, and even in democratic societies by being more persuasive than the competitors. Persuasiveness is not always related to the capacity to live up to the persuasion.

It has been suggested that a certain random element in the selection of people for powerful roles might well be better than a more deterministic system. The Greeks are supposed to have selected certain powerful people by lotteries, done by drawing their names out of a hat. There tend to be elements of this in democratic processes and institutions. A person rises to power in a democracy by having a long run of good luck. It is like having a tossed penny turn up heads 20 times in a row. The random element in the selection of powerful people is likely to lead to better results only if the nonrandom elements are mainly perverse. It certainly can be argued that many of them are and tend to produce those unfit to rule. It has been argued that the extraordinary persistence of the Roman Catholic Church over the centuries, for instance, is not unrelated to the fact that there is a fairly strong random element in the selection of the pope from the cardinals. Occasionally, therefore, one gets a Pope Gregory VII or a Pope John XXIII who were able to give the church the leadership it needed at the moment.

Virtually all political systems exhibit considerable traces of oligarchy, even in the most democratic of societies. There is always a group around powerful people who both influence the powerful and often take over the powerful roles. These are the juntas in Latin America, the White House staff in the United States, a circle of trusted intimates who seem to surround every president, and, of course, the politburos of the communist countries. Perhaps the main difference between a more democratic and a more authoritarian society is the number of potential oligarchical groups. In authoritarian societies, like the communist countries, there is only one such group, whose power is rarely challenged and whose composition changes glacially and only usually through death. In democratic societies there are large numbers of potentially oligarchical groups, depending on who happens to have been around a newly elected president, and power is widely scattered.

Timocracy, the rule of the rich, as such is actually rare. Oligarchies frequently contain what might be called the "old rich." The new rich are usually too busy getting rich, largely through exchange manipulations rather than by actively participating in politics. In the United States, for instance, many studies have shown that while there may be a large potential ruling group—people who have a much higher probability of rising to positions of power than the rest of us—it is not easy to identify, and it is constantly shifting small groups within this that actually rise to positions of power. Ironically enough, it is in the communist countries that timocracy is perhaps the best description of the situation. Where riches arise as perquisites of political power, it is the "aparatchiks," as they are called derisively in the Soviet Union, who ride around in automobiles with chauffeurs, have nice houses and dachas in the country, special stores to shop at, and so on.

One situation that Plato did not seem to envisage was the rule of the military. Curiously enough, there is not even a word for this—one might invent "militarchy" or something like that. This has become extremely common in the poorer countries today. Even in democratic societies the highest ranking people in the military (for instance, the National Security Council in the United States) are always part of the oligarchical group, and a persistent part of it, with profound influence on policies, even though they remain constitutionally subordinate to the civilian power in the shape of the president, who is commander-in-chief. It is rare, however, for the president to exercise this power, as Truman did when he fired MacArthur. In wartime especially, the civilian power tends to become subordinate to the military.

On the other hand, the fact that the military constitutes a professional class with rather narrow interests—for instance, in winning wars—means that there is often a kind of division of powers between the military in its own sphere and the civilian government in its sphere. The military rarely, when nominally under a civilian government, interferes in things like economic policy, criminal law, or government regulation. When the military takes over an entire government, of course, as happened in effect in Argentina, Chile, Uruguay, and Brazil, the results are often disastrous because the military usually does not have the skills to run a civilian government. Consequently, it is apt to make disastrous mistakes in economic policy that actually impoverish the society that it is supposed to be governing, as has happened in Uruguay, Argentina, and Chile. Even in nineteenth-century Britain, with its vast military-based empire, the military very rarely intervened in any kind of civilian policy.

Until recent decades, the military, or what might be called the "war industry," which includes those people involved in supplying the military with weapons and other things, has been a fairly small proportion of the total society or economy. In the United States, for instance, the military was less than one percent of the economy in the early 1930s. It went to about 42 percent (which was a world's record) in the Second World War, and in the "great disarmament" that followed it fell to 3 or 4 percent. It was 14 percent in the Korean War and has been declining slowly ever since, until just recently, to something on the order of 6 percent. Adam Smith, in *The Wealth of Nations,* says, "Among the civilized nations of modern Europe . . . not more than one hundredth part of the inhabitants of any country can be employed as soldiers, without ruin to the country which pays the expense of their service" (1937: 657-658). Although it is the military that tends to get into the history books, we always have to remember that by far the larger part of human activity is peaceful—plowing, sowing, reaping; building roads, railroads, and cities; making consumer goods, enjoying art, theater, religion, and all the innumerable peaceful activities of the human race. Even the political system—that is, in the form of government—is historically a relatively small part of human activity, although it has risen to some 20 to 30 percent in the modern world.

It should be emphasized that governments, whether national states or local governments, are by no means the whole story when it comes to political organization and activity. All human organizations have a political aspect to them—even the family, as we have seen. As societies become more complex, we get such things as labor unions, corporations, churches, foundations, schools, colleges and universities, innumerable kinds of nonprofit organizations, and so on. All these organizations have to have some kind of political structure and political activity connected with them. Labor unions in the United States, for instance, have a great variety of political structures, ranging from the two-party democracy of the typographers to ruthless tyrannies and dictatorships.

Business firms include monarchies in the one-person firm. Then there are kin-based oligarchies in the family firm, which even the Dupont Corporation was not too long ago, although it is no longer this way. Then we have oligarchies, especially in the corporation, which sometimes, however, are challenged by shareholder revolts, so we may have competing oligarchies. At the other end of the scale we have organizations like the producers' cooperative, rather rare and not too successful in most capitalist societies, represented in a small way even in the Soviet Union in the Artels and in a much larger way in Yugoslavia, where nominally worker-owned, though not always worker-controlled, firms are the basis of the economy. Then we have consumer cooperatives, where the directors are nominally elected by the members who are customers. Then there are firms like the rural electric associations in the United States, which, again, have boards of directors nominally elected by the customers but which are usually oligarchies, customers being rather apathetic except under conditions of deep crisis.

Churches range across the whole gamut of political structure, from the highly participatory democracy of the Society of Friends (especially those meetings without even pastors) to congregational-type governments (where the congregation at least selects the pastor) to the more episcopal and hierarchical churches (where ministers and priests are selected by higher authority). Then in the Roman Catholic Church, the Pope holds something of the position of an absolute monarch in some respects, although all absolutes tend to be modified in practice. The boards of trustees of professional associations are sometimes elected by the membership out of a limited slate put out by the existing hierarchy, and sometimes even this formality is dispensed with. Foundations are often governed by self-perpetuating boards of directors, who themselves appoint new members on the death or retirement of old members.

One suspects that there is hardly any possible form of political organization that is not found among private organizations. Political scientists have been surprisingly slow to study this aspect of political systems, being somewhat obsessed by the state, which may not even be the most interesting political structure. The great difference, however, between the political structure of the state and private organizations is that private organizations operate mainly in an exchange environment or an integrative environment of contributions, gifts, and foundation grants. And while they may use a little threat internally, they exercise very little threat power toward outside organizations. There may be some exceptions to this, like the Spanish Inquisition, the Klu Klux Klan, or the Irish Republican Army, but these actually are rather rare. For the state, however, threat is an essential element in its existence and survival, and this certainly marks it as different from private organizations. The political structure of most private organizations is largely a matter of hierarchy and how roles at different levels of the hierarchy are filled. What hierarchies do, however, is very diverse. In private organizations the actual carrying out of threat is a minor element. In the state, however, it is fundamental. A great deal of the resources of a state are devoted either to producing capability for carrying out threats or actually carrying them out, either against its own citizens, as in the law and the tax system, or against people outside the state itself, as in the case of military organizations.

The activities of government can be divided fairly sharply into those relating to internal matters within the state and those relating to external environments that involve other states. The former involves such matters as taxation, expenditures, budgets, budget deficits, and the development of the whole structure of law and its enforcement in the courts. The traditional distinctions among the legislature, the executive, and the judiciary are extremely important in American thinking and the American constitution. Some kind of separation of powers is found in all stable social-democratic societies, but is rare in the rest of the world. Thus in military takeovers the legislature is abolished or suspended, and the executive, in the shape of the military command, passes all the laws. It is rare for the military to intervene in the civilian judiciary, although it is not unknown. Sometimes, as in the communist states or in religious dictatorships like Iran, there is a nominal legislature, but its powers are extremely limited and the executive—for instance, in the shape of the Politburo in the communist countries—has an effectual veto over any acts of the legislature. The legislature is more what might be called a "ritual of legitimation" for the executive than it is a power in itself.

In parliamentary democracies, especially as we tend to find in the British Commonwealth and in Scandinavia, the executive is actually appointed by the legislature and hence tends to be dominated by it. This makes it easier to get rid of an unsatisfactory executive, like a prime minister. The legislature simply votes the person out of office. A principle peculiar to the constitutional monarchies, although very rarely exercised, gives the constitutional titular head of state the power to dismiss the prime minister. The last notable example of this seems to have been in Australia in 1975, when the prime minister, Mr. Gough Whitlam, was dismissed by the governor-general, Sir John Kerr, whom he himself had appointed, who then proceeded to appoint the opposition leader, Malcolm Fraser, as prime minister.

In the United States the separation of powers of the executive, legislature, and judiciary, is guarded by the Constitution and is also a treasured element in the political culture. It is rarely challenged. The interweaving of the separated powers, however, is quite complex. The president has the power to veto acts of Congress and to appoint members to the Supreme Court, but he cannot overrule decisions of the Supreme Court. In practice the veto power over congressional legislation is exercised with considerable regard for what might be called the "political climate," although the exercise of it is by no means rare. It is a little ironic, indeed, that the American Revolution produced a system much closer to a monarchical society in the United States, even though the monarch is elected by the people, than the system in the British Commonweatlh countries, where the power of the prime minister is much less than that of the American president. There is, indeed, almost a "law of irony of revolutions"—they nearly always tend to produce what they were intended to oppose. Certainly the Russian Revolution produced a nonhereditary czar with far greater powers than the unfortunate Nicholas II, in the shape of Lenin and Stalin and their successors.

A very important part of the political system is the international system. This consists primarily of the armed forces of the world, what might be called the "unilateral national defense organizations," which each country has (except perhaps Costa Rica). At times these are significant internally, as we have seen, in military takeovers and in the use of the military to suppress internal revolts or to conduct a civil war. These occasions, however, are fairly infrequent, and on the whole nations have unilateral national defense organizations, like the U.S. Department of Defense, and its equivalent in the Soviet Union and other nations, mainly to deal with what they perceive as external threat. In the past these forces have been used to create empires. They still may be used to create or expand areas of hegemony. The great age of empire is over and virtually all the empires have been dissolved, with the exception of the Soviet Union and the People's Republic of China, which, in a sense, are still peculiar nineteenth-century empires, although they would not admit to this term.

The international system also contains foreign offices, like the U.S. Department of State, which send diplomats abroad and receive foreign diplomats at home and also conduct extensive search and information services regarding foreign countries. There are also organizations like the CIA and corresponding agencies in other countries, which indulge in spying, collect information that is supposed to be secret, and occasionally conduct assassinations, or conduct minor wars on their own, as the United States is doing at the moment in Nicaragua.

In addition, we now have the United Nations with its central offices located in New York and a large number of specialized agencies, such as the World Health Organization, the International Labor Office, the Food and Agricultural Organization, the United Nations University, and so on. Some of these go back several decades. They have been increasing in number fairly steadily until just recently. The United Nations has an Assembly that meets in New York, a Security Council of the five original great powers and representatives of ten other nations. It has intervened in a number of places—the Middle East, Cyprus, the Congo—with highly specialized armed forces for the most part from the smaller and less involved nations. Its total budget is minuscule compared with the budgets for the armed forces of nations, but it is a source of world legitimacy and a forum, and it has a potential for being more significant than it is now.

The international system as it spreads out over time and space seems to divide itself into four major phases. The first phase is that of *stable war,* in which war goes on virtually all the time between two or more nations. We have had this in Southeast Asia for over 40 years. The Japanese, the French, and the Americans have all had armed forces there. The Vietnamese fought among themselves and also against the French and the Americans. The Vietnamese are now fighting the Chinese and have invaded Cambodia, and are fighting the remnants of the Pol Pot regime. Thailand alone has stayed out of all this, apart from some border skirmishes. In this tragic part of the world hardly anybody below the age of 45 or 50 has ever known anything but an almost perpetual state of war somewhere in the region. Going back in history we find similar periods—the Thirty Years War in Germany (1618-1648), the Hundred Years War between Britain and France, many periods during the Roman Empire, and so on.

Eventually, however, people get weary of stable war and we begin to get periods of peace. This might be called *unstable war,* a situation in which war is regarded as the norm but is occasionally interrupted by periods of peace that enable people to recover, recoup, and prepare for the next installment of war. Israel and the countries surrounding it have been in this state since the end of World War II. War, however, impoverishes and peace enriches, so it is not surprising that the periods of peace get longer and we pass into something that might be called *unstable peace*. The boundary here is not too clear. The international system in the European-dominated part of the world had something like this between 1648 and the present. In this situation peace is regarded as the norm, but it is interrupted by wars, the object of which is to restore peace, of course on terms favorable to the victorious party. This is why the American Air Force can use the slogan, "Peace is our Profession," meaning, of course, unstable peace.

Since about the end of the Napoleonic Wars in 1815 there has developed a new phase of the system that rarely, if ever, existed before, which might be called *stable peace*. This is a situation between independent countries, none of which have any intention of going to war with the others and have no plans for doing so, at least in any active sense. This seems to have begun in Scandinavia between Sweden and Denmark, who fought each other for many hundreds of years and then after 1815 gradually got into a position where it was clear that neither was going to invade or conduct war with the other. This spread to North America sometime after 1870. It certainly did not exist in 1812, when Britain and the United States were at war on the Canadian boundary and Britain actually invaded New Orleans and Washington but then retreated. In 1817 came the Rush-Bagot Agreement, which disarmed the Great Lakes as a frontier between the United States and Canada, at that time a British dependency. There was a dangerous episode in the early 1840s about the Canadian-American frontier in the Northwest. "Fifty-Four Forty or Fight!" was the campaign slogan of President James K. Polk, and war could easily have taken place, as the British and the Canadians wanted what they called "Cascadia," which is now Washington and Oregon. However, good sense prevailed and the Forty-Ninth Parallel continued peacefully to the Pacific in the agreement of 1846 ("Oregon Compromise").

Another dangerous moment came in the Civil War, when the British almost intervened on the side of the South, but thanks to the Prince Consort and some people in Parliament this was averted. Then in 1871 the Canadian boundary was finally settled and disarmed. Similarly, after the Mexican War of 1846, in which the United States stole New Mexico, Arizona, and California, and with the Gadsden Purchase of 1853, the Mexican border was stabilized and largely disarmed, although not completely.

Then after World War II in Western Europe came the Common Market, partly disarmed frontiers with easy access, and certainly none of these countries had any plans to go to war with any other. The area of stable peace now includes Japan and Australia, although certainly not North and South Korea, and probably not the Philippines. We have unstable peace as between the Soviet Union plus its Eastern European satellites, and the United States plus its NATO allies. It should be noted, however, that not all the countries at stable peace are in the NATO Alliance. Japan and Sweden are not. The primary condition of stable peace seems to be that change in national frontiers is taken off everybody's agendas and existing boundaries are simply regarded as stable, except insofar as they might be changed by mutual agreement, which is rare.

In Africa 40 or so new nations were formed as a result of the abandonment of empire. Their national boundaries cut across tribes and languages and are the result of the accident of empire and the geographical ignorance of the Conference of Berlin in 1884. Nevertheless, with the exception of Ethiopia and Somalia and the nascent states of Namibia and Angola, there has been remarkably little international war in the last 25 years, although there has been civil war, as in the case of Nigeria and some others, and some small interventions. It is much too early to say whether stable peace has been achieved, but at least the peace has not been very unstable, and the national frontiers remain much as they were about 25 years ago.

The current deterioration of the international situation in the last few years, the worldwide arms race, and so on, is a complex phenomenon. Some of it must be attributed to the Russian invasion of Afghanistan, which broke the Iron Curtain that had been stabilized for some 35 years. A complicating factor here is that internal changes may bring a country into one camp or the other, as the Cuban Revolution brought Cuba into the Russian camp and as political changes such as in China, Egypt, and now in Guinea sent countries out of the Russian camp. This is potentially a dangerous situation, as it makes a condition of stable boundaries between the two camps much more difficult to ensure.

Above all this now hovers the spectre of nuclear war. It certainly has a positive probability. The feeling behind the massive buildup of nuclear weapons and guided missiles especially of the United States and the Soviet Union originally was a theory of deterrence, mutually assured destruction (MAD). Nuclear deterrence has been stable for about the last 35 years, since the Russians started developing nuclear weapons, but it can be shown mathematically that it cannot be stable in the long run, for to be stable in the long run the probability of the nuclear weapons going off would have to be zero. If the probability of their going off were zero, they would not deter anybody; it would be just the same as not having them. Historically, systems of deterrence have always broken down. Stable peace is not a system of deterrence, as it is a system that has nothing to deter. There is overwhelming evidence now for the proposition that stable peace is the only stable kind of national security. The traditional national defense has become the enemy of national security and can only lead to national destruction, and perhaps the destruction of the whole human race or even the whole evolutionary experiment on earth.

Studies of the impact of even a fairly limited nuclear war, in which not all the existing nuclear weapons get exploded, suggest that this could cause such drastic changes in the physical and biological state of the earth that it would be an unprecedented evolutionary disaster. Jonathan Schell suggests that because of the radiation effects on the destruction of the ozone layer, life could very well go back to grass and cockroaches, which are less susceptible to radiation, and that no vertebrates or trees would survive. Carl Sagan and other scientists have suggested that a nuclear exchange would create such a massive dust cloud over the earth that nothing would grow for about four years. This would dispel the illusion of some people in the tropics that a nuclear war would merely devastate the temperate zones but leave the tropics unscathed. This, again, could lead to the extinction of all higher forms of life.

In this situation we have to distinguish between the intention of the people who control the system and the design of the total system. Thus automobiles are not intended to kill anybody. They are merely designed, along with the road system, to kill 40,000 people a year in the United States, perhaps 100,000 people around the world. Similarly, the U.S. Department of Defense and other unilateral national defense organizations are certainly not intended in the minds of the people who create and run them to destroy the human race and the evolutionary process; they are, however, designed to do this, simply because there is no organization at the present moment, outside of the condition of stable peace, that can diminish the probability of war to zero.

One of the great problems here is the problem of escalation. The U.S. secretary of defense, for instance, is talking about "limited nuclear war," which simply means that perhaps Europe and Korea become uninhabitable but the rest of the world survives in a state of perpetual ill health because of radiation. When one asks, "What are the institutions for limiting a nuclear war?" the answer is, "There are none." War is the breakdown of the taboos that constitute peace. In peace we do not do things we could do, like invading people, bombing cities, and so on; in a war we do them. War usually starts as a fairly restrained operation for destruction. If there is a rapid and conclusive victory of one side over the other, as in the U.S. invasion of Grenada, these restraints may not be broken. Almost universally, however, as one side feels it is losing it lets go some of the restraints and taboos. We saw this in World War II, which began with a "phony war," without civilian bombing for some six months. Then civilian bombing started and became more intense until Hiroshima, Nagasaki, and Dresden, which might be described as genocide.

The psychology behind war is a strange combination of hatred and love. We obviously cannot have war without denying the enemy and the most basic of human rights, which is the right not to be killed. This is justified in the name of the patriotism or the love of country. Perhaps as Samuel Stouffer (Stouffer et al., 1950) suggested, people both kill and die for their buddies rather than for their countries. It is the very close-knit integrative systems that develop under conditions of danger and stress that create this collapse of ordinary taboos.

Another factor in the situation is the dynamics of obedience. This is brought out very well in the famous Milgram (1974) experiment, in which subjects obeyed the psychologists, even to the point apparently of "killing" a person in the next room. Another factor is the growing impersonality of modern war. Where there is actual combat, with people coming face to face, there are strong tendencies for cooperative behavior to develop, especially among the ordinary soldiers, much to the dismay of the officers who are better trained in hatred and in the military morality. With guided missiles and aerial warfare, however, the perpetrator of these acts is far away from them. The man who dropped the bomb on Hiroshima was, for all intents and purposes, a pretty decent, normal American young man who would almost certainly have refused an order to throw a baby on a fire, yet had no hesitation in throwing the fire on thousands of babies because this was his role; this was what he was ordered to do. Military discipline is designed to destroy any independence of thought of the people who carry out the atrocities war involves. The My Lai incident in Vietnam was a good case in point.

To what extent can we say, then, that the political structures and processes of the world are a total system? Certainly these political processes are much less of a total system than, say, the economic processes. In terms of internal political structures there is enormous diversity, and even substantial changes in one country may not have much of an effect on others, although, of course, they sometimes do, as when an aggressive missionary regime takes over from a more relaxed and stay-at-home regime. On the whole, though, extremely diverse political structures can coexist with each other and even have little effect on each other. There will be effects, of course, on the world economy. If we get a political regime that is highly protectionist and hostile to the outside world and to world trade, the volume of world trade will diminish somewhat. Burma, for instance, has isolated itself from the world to a considerable extent since it became independent. Japan in the Tokugawa regime isolated itself from the world for almost 250 years with one small connection with the Dutch and the Chinese on an island in Nagasaki Harbor. In spite of this fact, Japan was profoundly affected by what was going on in the rest of the world, even in that period. The fact that it had fairly stable internal and external peace during that time led to economic and even cultural development far beyond the intentions of the shogunate.

Threat systems do not seem to have the long-run survival value that exchange and integrative systems do, simply because they do not pay off very well. The abandonment of empire resulted partly from the realization that empire was almost always an economic drain on the imperial powers and that countries that did not indulge in empire, like Sweden, found it much easier to develop than the great powers. Partly, also, the collapse of empire has been the result of its nagging hypocrisy and inconsistency with the political ideals of democratic societies. Hypocrisy, as we have noted, is a great source of social change in the long run.

When it comes to the international system, of course, the world is very much a total system and has been becoming so since the expansion of Europe in the sixteenth century. Even in the eighteenth century most European wars (for instance, between Britain and France) were conducted in North America, India, and various places around the world. As soon as we got worldwide empires, we got worldwide war. With the tremendous diminution in the cost of transport, both of goods and of instruments of destruction, the world has shrunk to an alarmingly small space, which has totally destroyed traditional national security. Security depends to a considerable extent on there being a high cost of transport of the means of destruction. This cost of transport introduces the principle of "the further, the weaker"—that is, the further an armed force is from home, the greater the cost of sustaining supply lines, often through hostile territories. As both Napoleon and Hitler advanced into Russia, the invaders got weaker as they were further from home, and the Russians got stronger as they were closer to the home base, until finally the invasion ground to a halt before conquest. It is a fundamental principle that what can be defended with weaponry depends on the range and the deadliness of the means of destruction. This is why gunpowder destroyed the feudal system, and why the nuclear missile must destroy unilateral national defense, just in the interest of national security.

What this means in terms of the overall political system of the world is hard to say. There are those who argue that only world government can solve the present crisis. There is some doubt about this, simply because of the relatively high incidence of civil war. It is clear that a federal government did not prevent the United States from having a civil war. Indeed, sometimes governments actually incite civil wars and make them more probable. If the United States had divided into two countries, North and South, at the time of the Revolution, it is doubtful whether there would have been a war between them over slavery. Each would have continued in its own way and the South would have eventually abandoned slavery in just the way Brazil did, as it became clear that it was uneconomic and inconsistent with the larger movement in morality and our knowledge of genetics.

The whole question as to the optimum size of the political unit is unsolved. There is some evidence that small countries manage their affairs better than large ones. Thus it is hard to see any advantage in a union of the five Nordic countries. Each manages its own affairs pretty well. Even within the communist countries, Yugoslavia and Hungary manage their economies much better than the Soviet Union does. One source of the success of the United States is the relative insignificance of federal government in terms of civilian government compared with the states and local government. Outside of defense, the federal government absorbs only about 3 percent of the American economy in terms of purchases, whereas the state and local governments absorb 16 or 17 percent. Britain would almost certainly be better off it if was less centralized; so would France.

On the other side, we have examples like El Salvador, Kampuchea, and Lebanon, which are small countries that have gone into a nightmare of cultures of violence and the disintegration of all political processes. It is clear that what constitutes the optimum size of the political unit depends a great deal on the nature of the political culture itself, and it is difficult to make any large generalizations about it. Nevertheless, there is a legitimate concern for preserving cultural variety, which is seriously endangered at the moment. Because of the enormous spread of the "superculture" of airports, automobiles, fast food establishments, blue jeans, and the like, many local cultures, which have great virtues, are seriously endangered.

It has been suggested that perhaps the ideal world, politically, would be a world of 500 independent states at stable peace, each with a distinctive culture and a great deal of trade and interaction between them, but not enough to destroy their identities. This could almost be called a "gardens with walls with doors" view of the world—a large number of gardens, each a national state, with walls around them so that they have some sense of identity and security, and yet with plenty of doors in the walls so there can be communication and trade between them. Perhaps this is a dream of utopia, but, as we shall see in Chapter 8, utopian dreams historically have had a profound effect on human life.

It is too easy to express the present situations in terms of the choice between one world or none. We are moving toward a unified world system with almost frightening rapidity, and it may be that one of the most important questions the human race will face in the next 100 years—assuming that we do not destroy ourselves with nuclear war—is how to preserve variety of culture, language, custom, architecture, food, and so on. We may not be able to preserve variety on the basis of geographical location, in which case we will have to preserve it with cultural enclaves and groups. The spread of Chinese, Indian, French, and other national restaurants around the world is an indication about how variety may actually be increased in a given area of a city, perhaps at the cost of lessening the variety of the world as a whole. These are questions that are well worth thinking about, even in somewhat utopian terms, especially if we try to evaluate the overall change in the state of the world.

CHAPTER 7

The World as
a Communication System

Communication is a phenomenon of outstanding importance in social systems. It becomes increasingly important as we move through time in both biological and societal evolution. There are even some parallels to it in physical systems—its importance there depends a little on how we define it.

Communication is a complex concept. Indeed, it is a cluster of concepts with poorly defined edges, but this very complexity adds to its significance. Perhaps the broadest definition would be that it consists of any process that transfers some kind of significant structure or pattern from one system to another. The word "significant" here perhaps makes even this broad concept a little fuzzy, for the question of significant for what or for whom is not always easy to answer. In the broadest sense we might simply define it as significant for the evolutionary process. Then we still have to answer this question: What is the evolutionary process? These difficulties arise because we have a strong sense that communication has to be "about" something and that we could have transfers of structure and pattern that are not about anything but that are significant.

Physical systems are the agents of communication. Certainly without them there would be no communication. Communications may be coded in either energy or matter, and we see this, for instance, in the phenomenon of human conversation and in spoken language. The speaker has some structure that is perceived in the form of images in the mind and no doubt coded in some energy and matter structures in the brain. This structure is translated to structures in the nerves that run down to the vocal cords. Here it is translated into motions of the vocal cords, which translate it into air waves, which are partly matter, partly energy. These air waves hit the eardrum of the listener and are there translated into patterns of nerve impulses, mostly electrical. These pass into the brain of the listener and are translated there into images that are unlikely to be identical to the images in the mind of the speaker but, if the conversation is successful, will be very similar to them. These images will produce a change in the structures in the mind of the listener, who then becomes the speaker, and the whole process is reversed, ending in the mind of the original speaker, who then may react, and so on. We are so accustomed to conversation that we take it for granted. Actually, it is a process of almost literally inconceivable complexity in terms of communication and change of structures.

In physical systems themselves perhaps the closest parallel to communication is in the phenomenon of catalysis. Here some chemical structure, the catalyst, has on its surface a pattern that acts as a kind of template attracting atoms in the environment to form a compound of different chemical composition, but of somewhat the same structural pattern as the template itself. This compound then goes off into the environment and another one may be formed. In the absence of the catalyst the newly catalyzed compound would still be stable, but the probability of it forming would be much lower, simply because the probability of this particular configuration of atoms actually coming together would be much less probable. Whether there are phenomena like this at the level of subatomic physics I confess I do not know.

With the coming of DNA and life, communication processes become much more important. The DNA molecule itself can be regarded as a self-catalyst that is able to attract chemical structures, molecules, and parts of molecules (ions) from its environment and build a replica of itself, at least in the form of a mirror image. This can then split off and repeat the process to create a replica of the original DNA molecule. In a sense, therefore, we can say that the DNA molecule communicates its structure to the new DNA molecule.

Communication does not end, however, with the mere replication of the DNA molecule, such as happens in cell division. When DNA molecules are assembled together in chromosomes and these are combined in the whole genetic structure of the genome, such as we find in the fertilized egg or even in the just-divided cell, this structure has a property that can be called, perhaps a little metaphorically, "know-how" (see Chapter 3). It is able to capture energy, in this case probably chemical energy from its immediate environment. It is able to select chemical structures from its environment and use energy to build these into more complex structures, which eventually constitute the living organism that it "knows how" to make. The exact process of "morphogenesis" by which, say, the egg becomes a chicken, and still more how the human fertilized egg becomes a human being with its almost inconceivable brain, is still a mystery, but clearly there is a communication here between some kind of structures in the genome and its environment that transfer information from the genome into the structures that it builds. There must be some structure in the genome, for instance, that enables us at the appropriate time in the development of the fetus to transform cells into blood cells, liver cells, or brain cells, which then, of course, may reproduce themselves through cell division. But mere cell division would never produce a cell of another kind unless the genome has the capacity to communicate.

The most elementary concept here is that of information in the technical sense of information theory. Unfortunately, the word "information" is also used for other more complex phenomena, so there is likely to be some confusion in language here. "Information" in the information theory sense is defined essentially in terms of a measure of improbability of a structure, which is also a measure of one aspect of its complexity. The basic unit of information is the "bit," which stands for "binary unit"—that is, a state or a system that has one chance out of two, or a 50 percent chance, of happening or existing. Tossing a coin is a good example. Traditionally most coins have something like a head on one side and some other pattern on the other, which is by analogy called a "tail." If we toss a coin, the chance of it coming down and landing with either the head on top or the tail on top is each about a half or 50 percent. This is the binary unit or bit. The chance of two coins both showing heads is a quarter or 25 percent. This represents two bits. Three coins showing heads would be three bits, and so on. The probability of a structure of three bits is then one eighth, or 12.5 percent. This logarithmic definition is convenient for many purposes, but it must always be remembered that the improbability of a structure increases much faster than the number of bits. The structure of a hundred bits has a probability of $\frac{1}{2}^{100}$, which is very improbable, indeed! Putting the matter in another way, the structure of 100 bits means that it is one out of a possible 2^{100} structures, each of which has an equal probability of happening (and 2^{100} is about 1268 trillion trillion trillion).

Information theory has been particularly useful to telephone companies because they are in the business of transferring complex structures from one mind into another, essentially in the form of conversation, except that instead of only airwaves being the intermediary between the vocal cords of the speaker and the ear of the listener, there is the intervening system of electrical impulses from one telephone mouthpiece to another telephone earpiece. The problem is how to code the information structures that hit one telephone from airwaves and have them emerge from another telephone that may be halfway around the world in the form of airwaves that are similar enough to the ones that went in the first telephone so that the message can be understood by the listener. Ideally, the airwaves that come out of the listener's telephone should be identical to the ones that go in at the speaker's telephone. If this is the case, then the wave or time patterns that go into the speaker's telephone and are transmitted by electrical impulses—or maybe laser beams or whatever the communication channel is—to the listener's telephone would be identical in structure. If they are identical in structure, of course, they would have the same number of bits.

Bits, however, are only the most primitive elements of communication. We see this in phenomena like simultaneous translation. One language goes into the ear of the translator and another language emerges out of that person's mouth. In terms of bits per second, the two flows of airwaves could be identical but the structure would be very different. We see a similar problem in the information in the fertilized egg. With the genome we might have two fertilized eggs with the identical number of bits. One has the potential for producing a hippopotamus and the other, a giraffe. The structures are obviously different. Structures, however, cannot really be measured in terms of a single number because they are multidimensional, and even if they could be reduced to numbers, which they may be, this is not a single number but an enormous set of numbers that cannot be reduced to a single number.

Communication, even in biological systems, cannot be reduced to the simplicities of information theory. Social systems involving human beings involve even greater levels of complexity because of the phenomenon of consciousness and what might be called "know-what." The fertilized egg certainly has something that can reasonably be called "know-how," in the sense that it knows how to make the appropriate organism. It seems unlikely that it has any "know-what"—that is, that it knows what it is doing. Even at the human level there is an important distinction between know-how and know-what. A good tennis player knows how to hit a ball over the net. Unless he is something of a mathematical biologist, however, he does not have the know-what that underlies the know-how. He is subconsciously solving differential equations, perhaps up to the third degree, as he observes where the ball is coming from and predicts where it is going to be in the next fraction of a second. His nervous system is able to inform his muscles to go through the exact motions that will enable him to hit the ball at the right time at the right angle. He certainly does not know how this is done in the nervous and muscular system; he just knows how to do it.

There seems to be some emergence of rather primitive know-what in the higher animals. There is certainly a learning process in what has been called "noogenetics"—the transmission of learned structures in the brain (or wherever they are) from one generation to the next by a learning process. Before the human race, not much of this involves conscious knowledge of the systems involved. It is more like the learning of an unconscious skill or a change in the stimulus-response patterns. With the human race, however, we pass into an enormously enlarged system of communication as a result of the capacity of the human mind for very complex images and for language, signs, and symbols that transmit these images into other minds. This enormously expands the field of significance of communication, into conscious understanding and knowledge, and also into evaluative structures, what we might call "know-whether." The capacity for imaging and the capacity for language are, of course, closely related. It would be impossible to have one without the other.

Language, however, is not the only form of communication. It is stretching language only a little to say that the universe "communicates" with the human race through the knowledge potential it transmits by the information that reaches us through the senses. It is perhaps poetic exaggeration to say that the stars communicate with us. They do communicate to us by means of light waves, infrared waves, and other parts of the electromagnetic spectrum in the form of energy, and we transform these structures of information into knowledge—that is, images in our minds that we believe correspond to the structures out in the universe. Science has added enormously to this process, not only through the communication among human beings about theoretical structures but also by an enormous enlargement of the sensing capabilities of humans through instruments such as the telescope, radio collectors, and the like. Similarly, the microstructure of the world in terms of atoms, protons, electrons, and the whole range of subatomic particles communicates to us because we are able to interpret the information they give off (translated into human sense data by apparatus) into images we believe correspond to the external structures.

An interesting question has arisen in the twentieth century in things like the Heisenberg Principle and quantum theory as to whether we can receive information from the universe without changing the universe itself. This is where the act of asking a question changes the answer and raises interesting questions about the role of information and knowledge. There is a famous story told to illustrate the Heisenberg Principle: A doctor asked a hospital patient how he was and the patient said, "Fine," and the effort killed him. This is a very general principle. When the communication is part of the system we are communicating about, then communicating about it will change the system itself. The social sciences are full of Heisenberg Principles. We try to find out a person's opinion by giving him or her a questionnaire, and the act of filling out the questionnaire alters his or her opinion. Predictions, if they are believed, can be either self-justifying or self-defeating. If a respected authority says prices are going up and people believe it, then prices will go up as a result of the prediction. A good example of the self-defeating prediction is found in the Book of Jonah. Jonah the Prophet predicted that Ninevah would be destroyed if it did not repent, so it did repent and was not destroyed, much to Jonah's annoyance. The Club of Rome predictions of impending resource exhaustions, or the predictions of nuclear disaster, may, one hopes, have similar effects.

The role of communication in all social systems is very large and has been constantly expanding. The development of written language was a tremendously important step forward in the development of a world communication system. It greatly expanded the range of communication in space, from the range of the human voice to the range of a carried written message. It is also greatly improved the record of the past because written messages can be copied, like DNA, and it also enabled the past to communicate with the present, although the present could not communicate with the past. The written record of the human race, as we find it in the great libraries, is a precious heritage of communication and profoundly affects the content of what we have to communicate about. Indeed, we stand on the shoulders of the past through its records.

Writings that have become sacred have a special influence on the communication system. The Bhagavad Gita, the Sutras, the Bible, the Koran, the Adigranth of the Sikhs, and even Marx's *Das Kapital* and the Book of Mormon in the nineteenth century all have a symbolic value that makes their influence far greater than the works of most secular philosophers. Even political sacred texts, like the Magna Carta in England or the Declaration of Independence and the Gettysburg Address in the United States, resound through the succeeding centuries.

The invention of printing had an enormous impact on the world communication system simply because it was cheap. It could reproduce words very much in the way DNA reproduces itself by producing a mirror image of the text with a letter press and then having that in turn form a mirror image of itself that reproduced the original text on paper. From printing came newspapers, which have had a great influence on the whole communication system because one person with something to say could now communicate with many. People also began to have an image of what was happening in the world as a whole, whereas previously they only knew what was happening in their own backyard. The development of communication as a total world system owes a great deal to the press and to magazines and journals.

Printing has also had a tremendous impact on the educational system of the world. A good textbook is used all over the world and creates a common culture among those who study it. There would be no scientific community of the kind we have today without schools, colleges, universities, libraries, and textbooks. Now radio, television, records, and videotapes bind the world into a still more unified system of communication.

The world educational system, especially at the college and university levels, begins to approach a total world system, although there are regional, national, and linguistic differences. It is not surprising that the largest department in most Russian universities is the department of Russian, or that English is a big department in English-speaking countries. Nevertheless, education transcends language. There are some countries, like Japan, that translate extensively and are very much part of the world culture. Others are much more isolated and language is a real barrier. At the level of graduate education, however, the world is much more of a total system. What goes on in graduate schools around the world is more similar than what goes on in the primary grades, although even there the learning process is much the same, even if the language, the geography, and the history that is learned may be different.

One would like to see developed all over the world a curriculum that would include a course on "The World as Seen from Where I Am." We have no reason to be ashamed of perspective. Indeed, it has survival value—that the lion that is just about to eat us should look much larger than the one that is a mile away. Or that those who are near to us should be dear; otherwise, there might be no children raised to perpetuate the species. Nevertheless, we recognize also that perspective is a necessary illusion—that the lion a mile away is in fact as big as the one that is about to eat us, and that the remotest member of the human race is as important to it as are our own children and loved ones. Such a curriculum in schools around the world perhaps could save us from the pathological forms of nationalism and ethnocentrism and release us to enjoy them in their healthy forms.

Communication patterns are dominant in organizational structures. An organization chart, for instance, is largely a diagram of who communicates with whom. Several types of communication may be identified. There are, for instance, "orders" in which a member of an organizational hierarchy at a higher level communicates to one at a lower level that something must be done. Ordinarily, the one at the lower level obeys. Then there are "messages." Messages usually go from a lower level of the hierarchy to a higher level. They are intended to change the recipient's image of the world in the direction of the image of the world possessed by the sender. In all organizations there is a process of message filtering by which only a certain portion of the messages that arrive from below at one level are passed on to the next. On the whole, communication from the outside world tends to arrive at lower levels of the hierarchy—the foot soldier, the sales clerk, the parish priest, the instructor—and its gets filtered (and often distorted) as it goes up through the hierarchy to the top. Similarly, orders get changed as they go down the hierarchy to the bottom, where they are carried out.

Increasingly messages come in from specialized message makers—from research organizations, from economists, from marketing research people, and so on—who are specialists in the knowledge of larger systems and larger environments. They convey this knowledge and messages to the upper members of the hierarchy. This is one possible way to avoid the great dilemma of organizational communication, which is that the lower members of the hierarchy often send messages to the upper members tilted according to what the lower members think the upper members want to hear rather than what the lower members perceive as truth. There is a tendency for the bearers of bad news, even when the bad news is true, to have a rough time. The development of a market in messages may be at least a partial answer to this problem, but even here the question of dependency is a real one. This is perhaps why top executives read things like the *Kiplinger Letter* and *Newsweek*.

A good many of the messages and orders in an organization, particularly a firm or economic organization, relate to processes of production, and here there is a certain parallel to the communication problems that are involved in the formation of biological organisms from their genomes. Production is always how we get from the genotype to the phenotype, from the chicken to the egg, from the blueprint to the building, from the idea to its realization in a product. In all these processes communication plays a crucial role. The automobile can be seen as a result of a very complex process of communication, from the designers, architects, engineers, planners, down to the assembly line, machinists, assemblers, and sales people.

Besides the order and the message there is also conversation—that is, a sequence and exchange of messages. There is some tendency for conversation to be confined to single levels of a hierarchy, with very little conversation between the levels. This can sometimes be dangerous. The capacity for a person ordered to do something to answer back, to say "I think there is something wrong with this order," can sometimes be important. The capacity of the person who receives a message also to answer back and say, "Are you quite sure this message is right?" may be very important. Within the board of directors there may be a good deal of conversation, but this rarely spills outside.

The political process also involves orders, messages, and conversation, but here the conversation can become much more extensive, especially in democratic societies. In a dictatorship there is very little conversation, only orders and distorted messages. In a democratic society conversation takes place between the rulers and the ruled through pressure groups, publicity, elections, and the like. This takes place also within the governmental structure. Within the legislature, for instance, a great deal of conversation takes place, not only in formal debate but in the "corridors of power." We have not only log-rolling, or bargaining, but also even occasionally the exchange of ideas and stimulations to think. In the American system presidents have varied a great deal in their capacity to have conversations with Congress, but it is an important skill. With the judiciary and the legal system, there is perhaps less conversation, although even here if there is strong public opinion that the legal system is not functioning properly, this message will get back to it, in the long-run form of the type of people appointed to the judiciary.

An important aspect of the communication system not always recognized as such is the price structure—markets and opportunities for exchange. A price tag in a shop window is a communication to every passerby who sees it, saying, in effect, "If you give me this amount of money, I will give you this suit of clothes, or pair of shoes, or whatever item the price tag is on." Advertisements play something of the same role. The invitation to buy may, of course, be accepted or rejected. Competition is a phenomenon also involving communication on an extensive scale. I may not accept the invitation to buy in one shop window because there is one down the street that I perceive to be on better terms. The imperfection of the market, which economists have talked a great deal about, is partly a result of imperfections in communication, some of which arise out of the cost of communication itself. In any situation there is an optimum degree of ignorance at which it costs more than it is worth to know any more.

In both economic and political life, however, there is not merely the communication of information. There is also persuasion, which can easily take pathological forms. Advertising can certainly be divided into purely communicative advertising, of which the want ads are a fairly good example, and persuasive advertising, which is designed to change the potential purchaser's value structure in such a way as to induce an acceptance of the exchange offer that otherwise might not have been taken up. Sometimes this persuasion has very little to do with the merits of the commodity itself. It appeals to all sorts of extraneous values associated with sex or prestige, or even plain human gullibility.

We see the same thing in political life, in that a great deal of communication from candidates for office to the electorate is of a persuasive rather than an informative nature, and, as we learn often to our cost politically, what is most persuasive is not always the most wise in light of subsequent events. The whole question of the role of regret in a communication system is very interesting. A communication that creates a regret for past decisions can be extremely powerful. Nothing destroys legitimacy so rapidly and so completely as a perception that we have been deceived, and deliberately deceived. There is some hope in this, for it does mean that deliberate deception frequently has an adverse long-run payoff to the deceiver, but unfortunately the long run can often be uncomfortably long.

The failures and breakdowns in the communication system are seen in a great many aspects of social life. We see this situation in the family, where in spite of the closeness of the relationship of the people inhabiting the same house and the constant contact with each other, there is often a great deal of cumulating misunderstanding, simply because so many things are taken for granted and are not talked about. The family relationship is one of reciprocity rather than exchange. Each member gives up certain things for the family and receives certain things from the family. The perception of the "terms of reciprocity" are very important—that is, how much each member perceives as being received in proportion to what is given. If one member feels that a great deal is being given and not much is being received, the family relationship is in danger. It is easy for each party to misperceive the perceptions of the others. In a simple exchange, the terms of trade—that is, how much each gets for a unit of what each gives—are so closely related to the price that the terms of trade are relatively easy to estimate, and the market might almost be called a public communication system. When the price of wheat goes up relative to other things, it is pretty obvious to everybody that the sellers of wheat have better terms and the buyers of wheat, worse terms. In reciprocity relationships, however, what one gives up is not necessarily what the other receives, so it is easy for communication to break down.

We find much the same phenomenon in the labor market and in relations between workers and employers. Here again, there is a good deal of reciprocity involved. The wage may be fairly standardized and in the public communications system, something that everybody knows, although even here there is a curious taboo on discussing wages and incomes, just as there is on discussing the more intimate details of family life. What the employer gets for the wage is, of course, the product of the work, and this is usually not sold directly, especially where wages are paid by the hour, but depends on the attitude and productivity of the worker, which is a reciprocity factor rather than exchange. Similarly, what the worker gives up in accepting employment is the contrast between the conditions of work and the work environment and the pleasantness or unpleasantness that may be associated with it, by comparison with other occupations, or even unemployment, and the employee usually does not know much about this. It is not surprising, therefore, that labor relations are often subject to breakdowns and strikes, which are a bit like a separation in a family. Firing or quitting has certain parallels to divorce.

There is an important role in situations like this for conciliators, mediators, and counselors, who act as intermediaries in the communication process, and so make the various parties' images of the situation somewhat more realistic. A spouse will often tell things to a marriage counselor, or even in the presence of a marriage counselor, that would not be said to the other spouse in the absence of a counselor. In fact, it is the business of a marriage counselor, in a sense, to renegotiate the terms of reciprocity, with each partner having better knowledge about the feelings of the other. Similarly, mediation and conciliation services in labor disputes have a similar function in improving the communication among the parties and producing more realistic estimates in the minds of each party as to what is going on in the mind of the other. Studies have shown that in labor disputes the labor representatives often have extremely unrealistic images of what is going on in the minds of the employers, and employers' representatives have similarly unrealistic images of what is going on in the minds of the workers' representatives. Sometimes in situations where there are several representatives on both sides, the representatives on the same side do not even know what is going on in the minds of the people on their own side. Here again, conciliation and mediation services play much the same role that a marriage counselor does in a marital dispute.

Without doubt the most pathological situation of all in the world communication system is in international relations, national defense, and war. This is primarily a threat system. It differs from the threat system of the law, however, in that the threats of the law against the criminal or potential criminal are fairly specific, although perhaps not quite so specific as they used to be. The law usually specifies within certain limits the punishment that is appropriate for each convicted criminal. People pay their income tax mainly because they have a pretty fair idea as to what will happen to them if they do not. This is deterrence at its most workable. In some other situations, such as violent crime, the existence of plea bargaining and a considerable variety of sentiments among both juries and judges make the outcome much less certain and the deterrent effect is weaker. The deterrent effect of the law depends on there being a fairly close relationship between the commiting of a crime and the threatened punishment. If criminals are not caught and if sentences vary greatly from one court to the next, the deterrent effect is greatly weakened.

In the international system the communication structure is extremely deficient. The price tag is a specific communication: "You give me so many dollars and I'll give you this article." An armed force is a very unspecific communication. It says, in effect, "If you do something unspecifically nasty to me, I will do something unspecifically nasty to you." It is not surprising, therefore, that deterrence in the international system has a constant tendency to break down into war. It has rarely been stable for long. Indeed, it can be shown (as in Chapter 6) that deterrence cannot be stable in the long run. If it were stable it would cease to deter. Thus if the probability of nuclear weapons going off were zero, they would not deter anybody. If, however, the probability is not zreo, then if we wait long enough they will go off.

Furthermore, it is easy for the same act to be interpreted differently by opposing sides in a conflict. An act that appears as purely defensive on the part of the party commiting it may be perceived as offensive by the other party.

There is a queer kind of negative reciprocity involved in the relations of two competing armed forces. The ostensible purpose of an armed force is to provide security for the country it belongs to. On the other hand, a sense of security in one country leads to a sense of insecurity in the other, which is what leads into arms races. These are frequently unstable positive feedback systems that arise out of the fact that the feedback communication is almost designed to be misinterpreted. What one country takes to be a defensive move the other one takes to be an offensive one. This accounts for the instability of an armed peace. It shows why stable peace is possible only in what is called a "security community"—that is, a group of nations, each of which sees its own security as a function of the security of the others.

The situation is made all the more dangerous and pathological by the relative absence of anything like a skilled corps of mediators, conciliators, and counselors, such as at least we have, to some extent, in the family and in labor relations. Diplomats are supposed to act somewhat in this capacity, although they are seldom trained to do so. Diplomats, in fact, are representatives of their own country. They are not expected to be impartial. The old joke about the diplomat being a man sent abroad to lie for his country is a little unkind, for there are many fine, honest, and courageous human beings in the diplomatic corps. Nevertheless, the role of the diplomat is not that of conciliation and mediation, and is not even that of supplying unbiased information to the rulers of his own country. The problem of corruption of information in hierarchical organizations, which we noted earlier, is also found sometimes in a high degree in the foreign information service of a government. Diplomats and foreign office officials are likely to filter out anything that seems like an adverse criticism of the policies of their own governments, and even to filter out any bad news that comes from a conflict. Espionage organizations are designed to an even greater extent to produce misinformation further from any kind of disinterested objectivity. There are, indeed, positive rewards for producing supposed information that is deleterious to the enemy and favorable to their own country. To be sent abroad to spy for one's country is likely to produce even more misinformation than to be sent abroad to lie for one's country.

Some institutions in the international system occasionally provide mediation services. Sometimes the rulers of one country will offer to mediate in a dispute between two others, as Theodore Roosevelt is supposed to have done in the war between Japan and Russia in 1904. The United Nations is the logical organization for activities of this kind, but it is seldom used. The Secretary General has on occasion offered "good offices" in a mediating role, and in a few cases this has been fairly successful, especially when coupled with United Nations security forces in trouble spots like the Congo (Zaire), Cyprus, or the Israeli borders. In direct diplomatic negotiations, however, the United Nations is little used and has hardly been used at all in disarmament negotiations, all of which remind one of marriage disputes with hardly a trace of a marriage counselor or labor disputes without a trace of mediation or conciliation services. It is not surprising that virtually all disarmament negotiations have broken down. They are designed to produce mistrust and misunderstanding and are an almost perfect example of the breakdown of the communication system.

As we have seen earlier, in the last few hundred years, and especially in the last 100 years, the world has changed from being a set of a considerable number of fairly isolated social systems with either no contact or only very occasional contact into something approaching a single social system. Changes in the technology of communication have played an overwhelmingly important role in this transformation into a single world system. This begins with the improvement of ocean transportation, the discovery of America by Europe; the later discovery of Australia and New Zealand, the Hawaiian Islands, and so on; the growth of world migrations across the oceans and of world trade. A significant part of this process was the communications that went along with it. Before Columbus, for instance, there had been no communication between the American continents and the rest of the world. From then on, increasingly each part of the world contained more and more human beings who knew things about other parts of the world because of the spread of communications. The foundation of the Universal Postal Union in 1875 symbolized for the first time the development of a world communication system among individuals. From that time on, any individual in the world could send a letter to an individual anywhere else in the world by the simple process of addressing it and putting a stamp on it. With the coming of the telegraph and the telephone in the middle of the nineteenth century and the laying of transoceanic cables, the communication system of the world again expanded to the point where today one can pick up a telephone and directly dial another telephone in a great many differents parts of the world. A few places are still fairly inaccessible.

Another very important feature of this period has been the growth of world fairs and world associations of great variety, especially those

I have called NGOs, which are nongovernmental organizations registered with the United Nations. We have some 4,000 of these, and the number has grown pretty steadily since the founding of the Universal Postal Union, although there were interruptions during the two world wars. The "world religions" up to the nineteenth century were pretty much confined to specific areas of the globe: Christianity to the Americas, Europe, Northern Asia; Hinduism to India; Buddhism to south and east Asia; Islam to a strip from Morocco to Indonesia; with innumerable tribal religions in Africa and to a lesser extent in Asia and Australasia. In the nineteenth century Christianity exploded around the world in the missionary movement. There is now probably no country in the United Nations that does not have at least one Christian church of some denomination. Hare Krishna, originating in a sect of Hinduism, is found all over the world. Boulder, Colorado is a world center for Tibetan Buddhism. Islam is pushing down into Africa. American Sikhs are found in many cities in the United States, and Marxists, while they concentrate in Eastern Europe and northern Asia, are also scattered all around the world.

Science, of course, is a worldwide culture of very active communication. When scientific communities are cut off from the world scientific community, as they were in China during the Cultural Revolution, they feel this very acutely. Just as there is probably no country without at least one Christian church, there is certainly no country without a school or college that exhibits the periodic table and teaches chemistry and physics. The world scientific community is not very well organized. Apart from the International Council of Scientific Unions in Stockholm, which is a union of the national academies of science, there is no world scientific association, although something like this may be in the offing. Nevertheless, world scientific communications are very intense through journals (there are now about 100,000), conferences, world "years" in various subjects, and so on. The same could be said of medical, engineering, and other professional associations of many kinds.

In the twentieth century we have had the development of radio and then television and the development of communication satellites and computer networks. Small transistor radios are now within the means of a large proportion of the world's population, even in the poor countries, and even though broadcasting is frequently monopolized by the state and listening to broadcasts or television from abroad in some cases may be illegal, it still is virtually impossible to stop the network, especially of short-wave radio, which is worldwide.

We are so much in the middle of the development of world communication systems that it is difficult to predict its consequences. But we must be careful not to exaggerate its consequences, for the world is not a "global village"—it just has too many people in it. The number of people any single person can communicate with is very limited. Still more limited is the number with which a single person can have a truly interactive conversation. It is important to recognize that communication is not merely the transmission of information but the development and transmission of knowledge structures. Information can easily become the enemy of knowledge when there is so much of it that it simply becomes noise. Information overload may result in a distortion of knowledge and the development of error. We still know so little about human learning, and particularly how it so often ceases prematurely and barriers are erected against any further information inputs that might challenge the existing knowledge structure, that we certainly cannot be sure about the relationship between information technology and human knowledge. There are at least some indications in the developed societies especially that the information explosion has led in some cases to an actual deterioration in the knowledge stock of the society. Television has led to a decline in the skills of conversation in the family and provides a learning environment of negative moral learning. What is learned, for instance, is that aggression and violence pay off, that ideas are not interesting, and that only the crudest of human emotions are worth practicing. At the other end of the scale, television certainly opens up a remarkable window on the world and provides an opportunity for learning we never possessed before. The expansion of human experience that is represented by the nature programs, for instance, where you can actually watch things happening in the world of the fields, the forests, and the oceans, of insect behavior beyond the range of the human eye, the great world of the microscope, the telescope, and so on, the incredible knowledge that we now have of the solar system that we did not have 20 years ago, thanks to space probes and artificial satellites, is something for which we can be grateful. On the other hand, a culture of learning can develop only under conditions of personal communication and conversation that puts a high value on the learning process and stimulates individuals to be self-taught, which is something we are still far from understanding and achieving. However, as the need for it is recognized, there is some hope of achieving greater cultures of learning in the future, particularly with all the opportunities opened up by the technological revolution in communication.

The communications revolution has certainly affected architecture around the world, tastes in food and clothing, music and art, and dancing, but it has had some tendency to erode local cultures. In architecture we see steel and glass buildings all around the world, even now in the communist countries, which still have a certain Victorian charm. Automobiles and airplanes are virtually universal and are powerful in transforming cultures and the appearance of cities. Even blue jeans and rock music are remarkably worldwide, particularly in the culture of youth. It may be that one of the greatest problems of the next century will be the preservation of cultural variety. The communications revolution has produced something that has been called a "superculture," which does seem to affect the local and peculiar cultures of places all around the world.

There is some hope, however, that even within the superculture we can develop a great variety of subcultures that is not possible in the small isolated culture, where almost everybody has to conform to the common cultural pattern. Thus it is not surprising that within the superculture there has developed a great variety of religious sects, sporting and recreational cultures, and so on.

Some have speculated that we are moving into an "information age" in which information will be the major product and communication the major activity of society. In economics this is reflected somewhat in the richer countries, in the decline in agriculture, which in earlier civilized societies was 80 or 90 percent of the population. Today in the United States it is only 4 percent. We should really add to that the supplemental agricultural industries, making the machinery and equipment, seeds, fertilizers, and pesticides that have enabled us to reduce the proportion directly in agriculture so dramatically.

Now a similar thing may be happening in manufacturing, which has been fairly stable as a proportion of the labor force. What has expanded as a result of the decline in agriculture has been government, service trades, education, and medicine, for the most part. Whether the development of computers and robotics will now cause a dramatic decline in the proportion of the labor force in manufacturing remains to be seen. It should be pointed out, however, that the information age really began three billion years ago with life, and that production has always been based on genetic information and know-how and communicated to molecules, for the most part, in the environment of a growing organism, in the case of production of biological organisms; and communicated to people of different skills and tasks in the case of human artifacts like automobiles. Thus in a sense all things are produced by information. There is, of course, the production of communications for their own sake in the arts, music, theater, dance, and so on, which also tends to be a somewhat increasing segment of the economy, particularly with the develop-ment of the phonograph and television and now of videotape and the Walkman. This has led to an enormous expansion of cultural communication. The number of people who heard a Mozart symphony in his lifetime could not have been more than a few thousand. In the last generation, the number is probably in the tens of millions.

An interesting but still unsettled question is that of the effect of computers on the communication system of the future. We are now moving into the age of mass computers just as we did into television in the 1950s and radio in the 1920s and 1930s. The computer has several significant properties. In the first place, it has a large memory, much larger than that of an individual human brain. It can store whole encyclopedias without much difficulty. The question of access to this memory is another matter. The human brain has an extraordinary capacity for what might be called quasi-random search and for recognition. The brain, indeed, is in the process of constant search all the time, even unconsciously. This is why it sometimes brings together, almost at random, highly improbable elements out of its memory bank in the formation of new ideas, or even poetry. Access to the computer is by rule and by rote, at least up to the present. If we know what we are looking for in the computer and how to search for it, we can find it, yet the great capacity of the human brain is to find things we are not looking for, or at least not looking for consciously. The human brain seems to be more like a codex or a book through which we can flip and catch what we are looking for or even what we are not looking for. The computer is more like a scroll, which can certainly be rolled and unrolled very quickly, but perhaps so fast that we cannot catch things on the way.

Another property of the computer is that it has almost infinite patience, unlike the human teacher, and this can be very valuable, especially in the teaching of those who are somewhat disabled or those who require patience. The computer can simulate conversation, but only in a limited way and according to a program. It does not have the extraordinary power possessed by the human brain of creating images in the mind. Even the computer translation of languages seem to have reached a certain block, and while the development of artificial intelligence is not necessarily impossible, it is certainly difficult except at an elementary level. A computer, essentially, is a very responsive moron, and an extended conversation with it would not have the same effect as a conversation with a human being, or even with a deceased human being in the shape of a book.

Another aspect of the computer is vulnerability. If complex structures are not to be vulnerable to malfunctions or breakdowns, they must have a great deal of redundancy, which biological organisms and the human brain certainly have but which the computer, on the whole, does not. (And it would be increasingly expensive to put it in.) If we come to rely too heavily on computers that do not have enough redundancy, then when they malfunction everything will go wrong—we will have a major disaster. We worry about this particularly in the case of computerized missiles, which undoubtedly increases the probability of almost universal disaster and greatly diminishes our security.

A final question regarding the communication system of the world relates to symbolic systems and the way in which these spread within the great ecosystem of the content of human minds. In language we make a distinction between signs and symbols. A sign is a communication that has some one-to-one relationship with what it communicates and the behavior that it induces. Road signs are a good example. When we come to a sign that says "stop," we stop, and then usually go on again. Even here, a sign that says "drive carefully" will produce somewhat different behavior in different people. On a larger scale, in religion, politics, and the arts, symbols refer not so much to something specific as to a general meaning of the total system. The search for meaning is a significant part of art, literature, and religion. Without meaning, indeed, the communications, as we saw at the beginning of the chapter, are not significant. The meaning of meaning, however, is elusive. It is the Holy Grail of philosophy—always sought but never quite found.

The power of symbols is one of the most puzzling things in human history. What symbolic power led to the monstrous religion of Moloch, in which people willingly sacrificed their children? In the future—if there is any future—we may wonder about the power of symbols like the flag, in the name of which perfectly decent people will commit unspeakable acts, such as the Holocaust of the Jews, the firebombing of Dresden, or the planting of bombs in Irish pubs.

Yet the love of country can be a very pure and noble ideal. In the name of the gentle Jesus Christians have not only slaughtered Muslims in the Crusade and persecuted Jews, they have also slaughtered each other from slightly different persuasions, as in the Spanish Inquisition and the Thirty Years War, and still in Northern Ireland. The major wars going on at the moment are within Islam. Hinduism has not prevented India from having one of the bloodiest histories of the human race. Buddhism, perhaps, has the best record, but even there Burma and Thailand had a long series of bloody wars.

It is perhaps the very ambivalence of the great symbolic systems that accounts for much of their power. This situation is often illustrated by the story from the European Middle Ages of "Buridan's Ass,"[1] the donkey between two equally attractive bales of hay—the question is, would he starve to death? The answer is no, because he wavers slightly and one bale would smell more strongly and he would go and eat that, then he would eat the other one. The donkey in this case is an approacher. On the other hand, if we put the donkey between two rattlesnakes, if he moves toward either one he would be driven back into the middle and would end up kicking and having a nervous breakdown. Suppose now, however, we put the rattlesnake on top of the bale of hay. The donkey moves toward it, lured by the hay, until the fear of the rattlesnake stops him. There he is stuck, an impotent captive of ambivalence. All the great symbolic systems have something of this quality. We are both drawn toward them and repelled by them, until we are captured by them. Perhaps this is why occasionally we have these strange replacements of one symbolic system by another. A new bale of hay with a small rattlesnake on it is presented to the donkey at right angles to the old one. He catches sight of it and escapes from his captivity by the one only to be made captive by the other as he approaches it.

It is essential to the understanding of the evolutionary history of the planet to recognize that it may have been dominated by the exact time at which highly improbable events actually happened. Even the physical world is not completely determined. The coming together of a group of atoms into a complex molecule, for instance, may be highly improbable, but if it is not impossible, it will eventually happen, and the same principle seems to be true of human history. Buddha, Jesus, Mohammed, and even Hitler were improbable events that actually happened. So, indeed, was DNA and the human brain. The more complex a system, the more the actual happening of improbable events dominates its history. We should not be surprised, therefore, that in the system of communication the creation of symbols should play a very vital role that is hard to understand, yet has to be accepted.

The religious experience of the human race is an important part of the world as a communication system, and the founders of religions have always been convinced that they were communicated with by some higher power in some other world, and this experience is common in the religious record. This is not, perhaps, so different from the way in which the universe communicates its structure and pattern to astronomers and cosmologists. It may be argued that the religious experience is purely inward and hence is suspect as a possible quirk of the human brain, whereas the astronomer's experience comes in the form of structure radiation from outer space. Still, the interpretation of this radiation pattern may also be a quirk of the brain, and in the record of religious experience there are several accounts of external visitations. We are left, perhaps, with the reflection that the world as a communication system is very complex, and that we see it only as in a mirror, darkly.

Note

1. The "ass" seems to have been a dog! See *Encyclopedia Brittanica, Micropoedia 1983,* Vol. 2, p. 382.

CHAPTER 8

The World as an Evaluative System

Evaluation is a central and constant activity of the human mind. It always implies statements of the form "**A** is better than **B**." It is expressed in ordinal numbers, like first, second, and third, rather than in cardinal numbers, like one, two, or three. It might be described as a quality rather than a quantity. It is transitive—that is, the statement "**A** is better than **B**" implies that **B** is worse than **A**. "**A** is better than **B**" means that **A** stands at a higher point on the scale of evaluation than **B** does. **A** is first; **B** is second in the order of what might be called "goodness." If **A** is better than **B**, it simply means that **A** is evaluated as higher on the scale of goodness than **B**.

An important aspect of evaluation is evaluation over time. If **A** is a state of some system today and **B** is the state of the same system yesterday, and if **A** is better than **B**, it means the system has improved. If it is worse than **B**, the system has deteriorated. Goodness, in this context, is what goes up when things get better and goes down when things get worse—always, of course, in somebody's evaluation, for evaluation is meaningless without an evaluator.

The process of evaluation is absolutely essential to the concept of choice. This is a concept that has been principally developed by economists, especially in the interpretation of what is called economic behavior. There is a curious difference between the approach of economists to behavior and that of psychologists. Psychologists tend to think of behavior as a response to a stimulus and think of it as a relationship between two events that they perceive as causal, at least in the sense that a given stimulus is supposed to produce a predictable response. Economists, however, think of behavior in terms of choice, a concept that perhaps depends more on introspection than it does on observation, and psychologists seem to have a strong prejudice against the introspective path to human knowledge about which economists have no inhibitions.

Choice is a process that originates in the perception of a set of images of alternative futures in something that almost has to be called a mind. These images, no doubt, are coded in some kind of structures in the human brain, although we do not really know how, except in simple cases. We can, however, distinguish different images of the future in our minds. In my own mind at the moment I have an image of the next half hour, which consists of continuing to dictate this chapter. I have another image, which consists of putting the dictaphone aside and making lunch.

These different images of the future, which might be called the "agenda of choice," are constantly being evaluated and reevaluated. Choice, then, consists of selection of that image of the future in the agenda which is "best"—that is, which is highest on the goodness scale—that is better than all the others. Then we initiate the corresponding behavior we believe will make the most highly evaluated future happen. At the moment, for instance, I am continuing to dictate, this standing highest in my evaluation or estimate of possible ways in which I can spend the next five minutes. When the five minutes are up, however, or I have reached some convenient stopping point in the dictation, it is highly probable that I will get up and make lunch, which is a future that at that point will have a higher value than continuing to dictate. This is what economists mean by the "theory of maximizing behavior," which is the view that in any matter of choice everybody decides to do what they think is best at the time. This almost might be described as a behavioral identity that hardly anybody will ever admit to the contrary. It is indeed a little surprising what an elegant set of mathematical variations economists are able to play on this very simple theme. Psychologists might want to say that the change in evaluations is caused by a change in the stimulus; for instance, if I finally decide to get up and get lunch, it is because of the stimulus of hunger or something of this sort, and stimuli certainly do change the agendas of choice all the time. But the response is not just an automatic effect of the stimulus as a cause. It is mediated through what psychologists call intervening variables—that is, in particular, the image in the mind of the agendas of choice, the ideas of possible futures, and the evaluations placed over these that may continually shift as the stimuli change.

In human beings evaluations get detached from choice and become an important activity of the human mind, almost for their own sake. We think of ourselves, "Am I feeling better in health today than I was yesterday?" or, after reading the paper, "Is the world better today than it was yesterday?" These evaluations, furthermore, are constant subjects of conversation. The commonest greeting that initiates a conversation is usually an inquiry into the state of the listener: "How do you do?" "How are you today?" or "How are things?" The response may be purely formal and conventional, like "Fine," or we might even make an evaluative answer, like "Much better," "About the same," or "Not too good," depending on how we interpret the inquiry. Subsequent conversation is apt to be punctuated with "What do you think of _____?"—meaning, of course, "how do you evaluate it?" Some conversation, of course, is simply informative, as when we ask somebody the way to somewhere, but a great deal is evaluative. Thus it seems a little absurd to suppose, as the logical positivists are supposed to have supposed, that valuations are so random and arbitrary that they cannot be studied, or are not really part of the world. It is clear that they are an essential part of the system of human life and interaction and that the social, economic and political systems cannot possibly be understood without them.

The record of the past suggests that there has been a certain evolutionary process in the direction of choice and valuation. Thus very early in the history of the universe we get chemical elements with valency and the capacity to combine into molecules. It is not wholly an accident that the word "valency" is related to value and valuation. We must not, of course, be anthropomorphic about atoms, but it is at least an interesting metaphor to say that carbon "likes" holding on to four hydrogen atoms in CH_4 (methane) and that CH_3 is a "radical" (again a metaphor) in that it is unsatisfied. Valency, of course, is a matter of the stability of particular proton-electron structures. The atom with two electrons, helium, is very stable; so is the one with what seems like an inner ring of two and an outer ring of eight, which is neon. Two hydrogens with one electron each and an oxygen with six electrons can form a stable ring of eight, which is H_2O, or water. Carbon has an outer ring of four electrons and hence needs four others to be stable, whether this is four hydrogens with one each or two oxygens with two each, as in CO_2. The fact that the clue to valency is the stability of certain configurations may have application in much more complex structures. Even human valuation is a search for some kind of closure or stable configuration of the immensely complicated patterns of the human mind. Chemical compounds may foreshadow in a very simple way the enormous complexity of institutions like marriage. It is certainly a little far-fetched to regard the oxygen molecule (O_2) as a homosexual union or carbon monoxide as prostitution, but different patterns of fulfillment do go all up and down the great chain of complexity.

As we move up to biological organisms we reach a level of complexity beyond that of simple chemistry but one also where there are certain parallels to valuation and choice, even at the level of the single-celled organism, like the amoeba. An amoeba will absorb a particle of food and reject a particle of dust. This certainly looks like a primitive form of choice, although one doubts whether the amoeba has anything much resembling a mind. Whether it has a mind or not, however, there is no doubt that it has preferences. Psychologists can say that it is just stimulus and response, when it rejects the dust and absorbs the food, but every stimulus and response pattern must have intervening variables, otherwise it makes no sense. Although the intervening variables in the amoeba may be much simpler than they are in human beings, they are still very complicated and have something to do with the organism as a total system, which includes what it seems not unfair to describe as a primitive form of valuation.

As we move up the scale of complexity in biological organisms, valuation processes become much more complex and closer to what we find in humans. Even in trees we seem to find chemical warning signals extruded into the atmosphere when something threatening appears in the environment. In plants preferences may be expressed much more in structure than in behavior. The structure of some plants invites a certain kind of pollenating insect and others do not. The enormous diversity of methods of scattering seeds suggests a kind of preference that is implicit in the genetic structure and, of course, derived from natural selection.

As we move into the animal kingdom valuations become more obvious. The unbelievable variety of mating behavior suggests that almost every species develops sexual preferences of its own, again coming out of natural selection of genetic mutations. Sometimes, indeed, the preferences that prosper within the species may lead to its extinction, as in the famous story of the Irish elk.

The evolution of pain and pleasure, which clearly seems to reach pretty far down in the animal kingdom, is a clear example of the development of processes of valuation. Fear and flight, again, are common evaluative structures and clearly have a survival "value." The very fact that we use the phrase "survival value" indicates that the process of selection always implies valuation of some sort. In the record, which suggests constantly changing environments punctuated by catastrophes, the long-run survival value of adaptability and redundancy is very clear. The evolutionary race is not to the strong but to the meek—that is, the adaptable. Mice and cockroaches seem to be the least endangered of all species. Specialization and adaptation prosper in the short run but can often be disastrous in the long run. Adam Smith saw that the division of labor—that is, specialization—in the human race could produce riches but also produced a corruption and enfeeblement of the human person that boded ill for the too-specialized societies. Here again, survival value is closely related not to the "fittest" (which is nothing but the surviving) but to the fitting, here again, those who fit into a structure that has some kind of closure or stability, just like chemical valencies.

It is significant, therefore, that although evolution has never produced a single evaluative system, evaluation processes permeate it from the earliest time. The multiplicity of evaluative systems, indeed, like the enormous variety of species of organisms, itself has survival value. If evolution had produced a single organism, a great dragon with its tail wrapped around the earth, it would simply have died and that would have been the end of the whole process. It is the very variety of the ecosystem and the variety of valuational structures it implies that has made evolution a continuous process, able to adapt and even thrive in the presence of occasional catastrophes.

Coming now to the human race and societal evolution, it is clear that humans produced a profound transformation in the evolutionary process itself. Humans may not be genetically all that different from chimpanzees, but the small genetic difference has made an enormous evolutionary difference in terms of the human brain, capable both of the formation of images, especially images of the future, and of complex valuational systems, orders of magnitudes greater than any previous biological organism. In human history evaluation and evaluative processes are supreme. The world ecosystem is increasingly dominated by human artifacts, and human artifacts are produced because somebody wants them, not because some biological gene insists on producing something, which is the case in the biosphere. The selective process now includes supply and demand, both of which are essentially valuational processes. In an exchange economy, if somebody produces some commodity that nobody wants and it will not sell, it will soon disappear. In centrally planned economies, if somebody produces something that the central planning agency does not want, it also will disappear (and probably also the person who produced it). Supply and demand rule both capitalist and communist economies, with minor differences about whose demand and whose supply is significant.

The question as to where human valuations come from is extremely significant. It is also puzzling. There is a little linguistic problem here, in that we are prone to talk about "values" as if they were things, whereas what is most significant are the processes of evaluation. Benjamin Whorf's hypothesis (1969)—that the structure of language had an impact on the substance of what language was trying to communicate—perhaps has some validity here. The Indo-Aryan languages, like the English language in which the original form of this book was written, because of their subject-verb-object structure of sentences, tend to overemphasize things and underemphasize processes. A famous example of this is the sentence "It is raining," when there is really no "it"; all there is is raining, a process.

Things are merely snapshots of sections of processes. The process is a more fundamental reality. We talk about "values" as if these were permanent structures in the human mind, whereas what we are really talking about is a kaleidoscopic shifting pattern of constant valuations. This is not to rule out the possibility that there are, in fact, structures within the human brain that could conveivably be called things, which help to direct and determine the processes of evaluation, but the brain seems to be almost as kaleidoscopic as the mind it encodes. Whether there are "values" sitting in the human brain and mind is a question hardly necessary to answer as long as we recognize the existence of the processes of evaluation, for this is what we have to try to understand.

An important, but at the present time almost unanswerable, question at the outset is the extent to which these valuation processes are built into the structure of the organism as a result of biogenetic processes of the original genes, and the extent to which these processes are learned. It is clear, of course, that both the genetic structure that creates the biological underpinning of the brain and so provides the potential for learning and the learning processes that realize this potential are significant, but how far the genetic structure limits and prejudices the learning of valuation skills is still an unanswered question. The learning process is so complex and so hard to observe, particularly when it involves things like imprinting and "readiness" as the genes expand the structure of the brain, that we have to admit to a great deal of ignorance. We have to recognize that there are certain perversions in the valuation learning process that produce people with depression and suicidal tendencies, for instance, or a total incapacity to empathize or participate in the lives of others and who tend to exclude themselves from the community of other human beings. But how far these things are genetic, the result of chemical malfunctioning, and how far they are learned, especially by the accidents of imprinting, we simply do not know.

There is no doubt that the physiological, and presumably genetically created, capacity for pain and pleasure, just as experiences, are tied in with evaluative learning. Even here the relationship is complex. Psychologists assume rather easily that they know what constitutes positive and negative reinforcements, and perhaps in rats they do, although I am not even sure of that. When it comes to human beings we have "the pain that is almost a pleasure and the pleasure that is almost a pain." We have phenomena like masochism in which physical pain takes on a high value and is desired, and we certainly have cases, as in monasticism, where sexual pleasure is shunned and given a low value. Again, there are those who eat to live and those who live to eat, with presumably much the same physical pleasures involved in taste and so on. In spite of Jeremy Bentham, the great philosopher of utilitarianism, human valuation is much more than mere physiological pleasure and pain, although these are important. On the whole, certainly, we prefer physiological pleasure to physiological pain, as every dentist knows. Much evaluation, however, is quite unrelated to physiological pleasure or pain and involves an evaluation of very complex images that have no impact on the pleasure or pain centers. We can say the same thing in the form that there is something we might call mental pleasure or pain, which is different from physical pleasure or pain, and a large part of our evaluation process concerns the former. That, of course, is where most of our valuation dilemmas come from as well.

Another little understood phenomenon of considerable importance in the evaluative system is that of conversion. Sometimes there is a sudden overturn in the system of valuations. Things that previously were regarded as good now become regarded as bad, and vice versa. Conversion can be religious or political. A similar phenomenon is falling into or out of love. The person who seems extremely attractive may suddenly seem to be quite unattractive, and, again, vice versa. It is clear that at some more extreme points in the system it becomes unstable and we get changes that can be described only by catastrophe theory.

The difficulty of identifying the learning process in evaluative learning and the role of genetics in it is illustrated by the phenomenon of homosexuality. If this had strong genetic roots, it clearly would not last very long, as practicing homosexuals are likely to have very few children. The genetic structure clearly must provide the potential for all forms of sexuality, simply because of the remarkable stability of this diversity within the human race. Homosexuality, therefore, must be mainly learned. But how? That, I think, nobody knows.

There certainly seems to be a strong tendency for the perpetuation of general value-evaluation structures in the family, which suggests that early childhood experiences have a great deal to do with the learning of what might be called "further predispositions" for evaluative learning. We see this in the tremendous importance of the family and in the transmission of religious cultures and even of political cultures. This is fairly understandable. What is more puzzling are the occasional epidemics, as they might almost be described, of conversion, when particular religious or political valuations or constellations spread through populations that previously held to rather different ones. The spread of Christianity, or even of subsystems within it, like Mormonism, or the spread of Islam or Marxism around the world, is a striking phenomenon and yet is little understood.

Evaluative learning is closely related to certain ideological structures and beliefs, particularly the nature of the larger systems of the world and the universe. This seems to be the case especially in the evaluation of religious and political practices. The role of monopoly in communication in this regard is important. The person who grows up never having heard anything else but the ideology and the evaluation structures of his or her family and immediate community or nation is quite likely to regard any contrary communications, if they are heard at all, as emerging from the alien and the enemy and therefore not to be regarded. Free competition among ideologies—as we see, for instance, in many countries now with the separation of church and state, as Adam Smith saw—tends to moderate them and develop a kind of ecumenical learning between them. Monopolies of ideology, however, are extremely adverse to human learning, especially when embodied in a strong political threat system.

No matter how it is learned and, to a considerable degree, no matter what its actual content, the evaluative patterns of the human mind exhibit a common general structure. In the first place, as we have seen, evaluation always involves an ordering in regard to better or worse of two or more images in our minds. These images can perfectly well be fantasies that we do not believe have anything corresponding to them in the real world. I might say, for instance, that Plato's *Republic* is a better society than More's *Utopia*, in spite of the fact that neither of them ever existed, except in people's minds. It is unfortunate that there seems to be no word, in the English language at least, for that which is evaluated, and one is tempted to call it an "evaluand." These evaluands may be of great diversity and vary tremendously in scope. They may simply be the pimple, as when we might say "The pimple on my cheek is better (or worse) today than it was yesterday." It may be our total state of health, it may be our riches or our prestige, it may be the state of the community in which we live, of the firm we work for, of other forms, of our nation or of the whole world.

Both people and cultures vary fairly widely in the scope of their evaluands. Some people are very narrow and rarely evaluate anything beyond the condition of their own body and mind or their own family and immediate neighborhood. Others, like the environmentalists, form strong valuations about the state of the whole world. There are very few people who worry about the state of the whole universe, or even of the solar system, although if we found there was a large asteroid heading for a collision with the Earth, we would certainly think that the state of the solar system had changed for the worse, or if a nearby star were suddenly to become nova deluging the Earth with harmful radiation, we would also think that at least part of the galaxy had changed for the worse. We can hardly be blamed, however, if the scope of our valuations never really goes beyond the planet in which we live. Even the most ardent environmentalists do not worry very much about the garbage that man has left on the Moon, even though this does mean that three or four billion years of virginity in regard to the human race are now ended.

Another universal property of the evaluation process is that the systems we are evaluating, the evaluands, are usually complex and consist of many parts, each of which we might evaluate, and we face the problem of how to sum the evaluation of the parts. Indeed, we see this even in the evaluation of our own health and state of mind if somebody asks us how we are and we reply, "My cold is much better but my arthritis is a little worse, so on the whole I am a little better than I was yesterday." Or we might say of a president of the United States, "His domestic policy is a little better than his predecessor's, but his foreign policy is so much worse that on the whole I think we are in worse shape than we were before."

A good example of evaluation proceedings of this kind is accounting. The most basic concept of accounting is that of the balance sheet and the net worth of a system, whether this is an individual person, a corporation, or even a nation. This is an evaluation of the state of the system at a moment of time. It starts off with a position statement, which is a list of all the relevant items that have to be evaluated. Each can be divided into assets with a positive value and liabilities with a negative value. This, however, is a heterogeneous list. It includes cash, bank deposits, debts to and from the person or organization in question, land, buildings, machines, furniture, goods in various stages of production. It may also include certain intangible things that often are not counted. Some accounting systems have included an item called "goodwill," which tried to take into account such intangibles as the reputation of the product, the nature of the competition, and so on. A list of assets and liabilities cannot be added up unless each item can be reduced to a "measure of value," which in accounting is always a monetary unit, like the dollar or the yen. This is fairly easy in the case of cash, a little more difficult in the case of uncertain debts, and much more difficult when we have to translate acres of land or buildings or machinery into some monetary unit. We do this mainly by referring to some market price at which the item in question has been, or is now being, exchanged. For instance, if an item is 1,000 bushels of wheat, in order to translate this into dollars, we have to know how many dollars per bushel. If this, say, is $4 per bushel, the 1,000 bushels is put down as $4,000. At $5 a bushel it would be $5,000. This can be called an "evaluation coefficient." This is usually derived in some way from the actual price at which wheat exchanges in some market. In a case where the exchange took place some time ago—as, for instance, in building a building—we usually have information on the costs at the time of construction. Then, however, we have to allow for depreciation of value. Most things, with the exception of works of art and antiques, decline in value with age.

A further complication is that the value of some things in the present depends on some expected future value. If one of our assets, for instance, is a promissory note that promises to pay us $1,000 at this time next year, how much should be accounted now? This is the problem of discounting over time and involves a rate of discount that is the rate at which the future value declines as we approach the present as we go backward through time. If this rate of discounting is, say, 10 percent per annum, $1,000 this time next year will be valued at only $909 (10 percent of $909 is approximately $91, which added to $909 is $1,000).

Then when the accountant has reduced all the items on the position statement to a number of dollars, he simply adds these up, plus for the assets and minus for the liabilities, and the result is the "bottom line," which is the net worth. There are many things, of course, that cannot be valued in dollar terms, except roughly. The principle by which we evaluate complex structures is much the same as the one the accountant uses. We have to make some kind of at least rough evaluation in terms of comparable units of the different items involved and then add them up, even if the result is only qualitative and very rough. This process goes on almost unconsciously in our minds when we are evaluating complex structures or making difficult decisions. In a decision to take another job or to move to another city, for instance, we balance all sorts of things in our minds. Some we put a high value on and some a smaller one, and almost unconsciously we add these up and come out with a total evaluation as to which of the possible futures we really prefer.

A phenomenon sometimes takes place here in this qualitative accounting, as it might be called, that is unfamiliar to the professional accountant but that is sometimes of great importance. This is what we might call a "negative evaluation"—that is, we concentrate on what we do not like about the alternatives rather than what we do like. This often comes out with a rather different answer than we would get if we concentrated on what we do like. Concentrating on the negative valuations tends to expand the liabilities and diminish the assets in our mind. People can almost be divided into approachers and avoiders—those who, in making decisions, concentrate mainly on what they do like and are attracted toward and those who concentrate on what they do not like.

This leads us into the problem of dilemmas—that is, situations in which two alternatives seem equal in value and therefore we cannot decide which one to choose. This is a problem that economists have completely neglected. They have always assumed that there is one alternative that is clearly better than all the others. Dilemmas, however, can be very painful, particularly where for each of the possible alternatives there is a considerable range of uncertainty of our evaluation of them and these two ranges overlap. Dilemmas can be costly and also can often lead to bad valuations and decisions that are later regretted. We have noted in Chapter 7 the dilemma of the donkey between two rattlesnakes and the ease with which he solves the problem of the two equally attractive bales of hay. This, perhaps, explains why radicalism is so often disappointing and frustrating. Frequently radicals are avoiders: They know what they do not like, but they do not really know what they do like. Hence radicals have a depressing tendency to destroy each other and often end up with ruthless dictatorship. On the other hand, moderate conservatism (middle-of-the-roaders who know what they do like much better than what they do not like) are often able to achieve substantial social change at much lower social costs than are imposed by the radicals. This is a subject, however, that has been remarkably little studied. We need to know much more about it.

For all evaluational processes, then, we can postulate a "goodness function"—that goodness, or the ultimate value, is a function of our estimate of the relevant state of the system we are evaluating and that this, in turn, can be divided into intermediate values, which might almost be called items in the overall balance sheet. These intermediate values are things like health, riches, justice, freedom, beauty, knowledge, wisdom, compassion—the list is very long. Almost all of these have negative counterparts: sickness, poverty, injustice, oppression, ugliness, and so on. The former can well be called "virtues" and the latter can be called "vices." Each virtue and the corresponding vice constitutes something of a continuum, although sometimes there is something of a break between them. Thus there is a certain gap between being perfectly healthy and even having a pimple. Sickness, however, goes from the pimple through degrees of seriousness to death. Riches and poverty are on a continuum, except there is a certain gap where poverty becomes destitution, utter misery. Each of these virtues and vices, of course, is itself an evaluation of a complex system, and there may be considerable divergencies in the evaluations of different individuals, particularly in regard to such things as justice and freedom. Even an average American and an average Russian, if such exist, would give very different answers to the question as to which countries are most just or most free. We will return to this problem later.

One complicating factor in the overall evaluation of a situation is that the virtues and vices themselves are related. Thus getting sicker often makes you poorer. As societies get richer it may be easier for them to be more just and freer, although there is some doubt about this. These interrelations have to be taken into account, however, and we cannot always simply assume that an increase in something we regard as a virtue will necessarily make things better. If the increase in the virtue is accompanied by an increase in a vice, or if a diminution in a vice increases another vice, it may make things worse. Prohibition in the United States was an interesting case. It certainly diminished drunkenness, which is a vice, but it increased crime and disrespect for the law, which are also vices, and the net result could easily have been adverse.

One of the great sources of errors in evaluation is the tendency we have to identify the intermediate values of virtues and vices as if they were ultimate goodness, and it is easy to make things worse with all the goodwill to make them better. Another source of evaluative mistakes again derives somewhat from negative evaluation—the belief that all we have to do is to show that something is bad and to get rid of it. Merely showing that something is bad, however, tells us nothing. We always have to know whether anything else is better. Something may be quite bad and may still be better than the alternatives, which are still worse. This, again, is likely to be an error of political activists, and especially what might be called the "one-cause" activist, who is interested only in diminishing a single evil without realizing that this may be diminished only at worse cost in the rise of other evils or the diminution of goods.

Again, we need to raise the question as to whether the evaluative system is indeed a total world system or whether it is simply a mosaic of rather isolated systems. As in the case of the other social systems, the history of the human race has represented an almost constant transition from a mosaic of isolated systems, such as existed in the paleolithic, toward the more integrated world system that we have today. This change accelerated spectacularly after the European discovery of America some 500 years ago and has accelerated even further in the last 100 years. Nevertheless, the evaluative systems of the human race are still very diverse. In a sense it can be said that each of the 4½ billion human beings on Earth today has a somewhat different system of evaluative processes, although these do tend to cluster within groups of various sizes. There is perhaps a certain underlying biogenetic dimension to the whole process that tends to unify it, and there are also a number of mechanisms by which different valuations are coordinated and affect the total system even though they are not identical.

The clusterings of value systems are along the lines of subcultures. The human race is divided into a large number of subcultures: tribal, national, occupational, religious, familistic, educational, and so on. It is one of the marks of a subculture that its members possess a value structure that is characteristic of the subculture as a whole, and that any member who diverges from this common value structure will either tend to conform to it, move toward it, or else will either be expelled from the subculture or will leave it voluntarily. A Jesuit who publicly announces that he has lost his faith, a member of a motorcycle gang who says he hates motorcycles, a university professor who puts no value whatever on teaching and research, a soldier who has become a pacifist will all find themselves very uncomfortable and will either leave the group or be expelled, or will conform, at least publicly, to the group ethos or valuation systems.

Many of these different subcultures are hostile toward one another. This tends to reinforce the ethos of each subculture and to prevent the development of a common ethos between the subcultures, although there is a curious tendency even for enemies to become more like each other, simply because each shares a culture of enmity that has profound effects on all the other aspects of the culture. This is one of the depressing things about the world evaluative system—that cultures of enmity and violence are more likely to spread and become characteristic of the whole human race than are cultures of tolerance and fraternity. Fortunately, this tendency toward cultures of violence is not absolutely necessary or inevitable; and increasingly, as violence has become ever more costly, the more nonviolent cultures have tended to spread, as we see in the development of stable peace between nations and in the development of tolerant democratic institutions.

The question as to whether the common genetic heritage of the human race, which is very large, moves us toward evaluation processes that have a lot in common is an interesting and somewhat unresolved question, as we saw earlier. Certainly every individual human being has a different genetic inheritance from every other, with the exception of an identical twin, but these differences are a relatively small proportion of the total genetic structure, and the common element is a large proportion of it. It is still uncertain how far the genetic heritage is responsible for the differences in valuations of different individuals. The evidence suggests that if genes are responsible, it is only for extreme cases and that in fact the common genetic heritage does incline us to an important common pool of evaluation processes. This is the "human nature" beloved of many philosophers, and it would be helpful if we knew better what it was and how we could appeal to it. What seems to emerge from human experience is that it can be appealed to but that we are not very skilled in appealing to it, especially because it seems to be the dynamics of human learning from each other rather than the genetic dynamics that inclines us to violence and hostility.

There have been attempts to attribute the violence-prone value structure of the human race to its simian ancestors, or even further back (see, for instance, Tiger and Fox, 1972). The evidence does not seem to support them strongly, and the common ancestors of apes and humans are about as likely to be peaceable, like the gibbon, as quarrelsome, like the baboon. Even in the apes we do not know how much peaceableness or quarrelsomeness is biogenetic and how much is noogenetic—that is, learned behavior that is transmitted from one generation to the next by a learning process with a biogenetic structure that is capable of many different varieties of learning.

Another set of processes that makes for integration in the world evaluative structure are processes that lead to the coordination rather than to the unification of different value structures. An important instrument of such coordination, often unrecognized, is the whole system of exchange and markets, which, as we saw in Chapter 5, has become increasingly a worldwide system, a process that has been going on for thousands of years and has accelerated remarkably even in the last 40 years, with a sixfold increase in the volume of international trade since 1945.

The market coordinates valuations by permitting individuals to satisfy their own preferences according to there own valuation structures without this diminishing substantially the possibility of others doing the same. That is, the market "economizes agreement." In a prison or commune everybody has to eat the same breakfast for the most part. When there is a market, those who like coffee and doughnuts can have them, if they can afford it, and those who like eggs and bacon can have them, if they can afford it. There is an old English nursery rhyme that goes, "My wife and I lived all alone in a little brown house we called our own, she liked coffee and I liked tea and that was the reason we couldn't agree," and the chorus, "Little brown jug, don't I love thee," suggests that they had solved the problem by each becoming alcoholic. If, however, there is a market, they do not have to agree, especially if the coffee and tea are instant and can simply be made by the cup.

The more sophisticated political processes, as we see them in the social democracies, also economize agreement because in a sense they are a political form of markets with log-rolling, influence groups, and all that. Also, the fundamental principle of majority rule rests on the assumption that minorities will not be pressed too far.

Under many circumstances, of course, these coordinating processes break down. Then we get the much less pleasant coordinating processes of tyranny and dictatorship, which means, of course, that everybody has to suppress his or her own valuations in favor of those of the dictator. Even the worst tyranny, however, ends in a funeral at which the sorrow is remarkably muted and the tyrant is delegitimated by a more tolerant successor, as Khrushchev did to Stalin.

Another possible method of coordination rests on the question as to whether there is anything in the field of human valuations that corresponds to "truth" in our images of "facts." The record of the history of human images of the world suggests that there is a certain instability in error, in the sense that if an image is in error, it is more likely to be changed simply because the error will eventually be found out by some kind of testing. The extraordinary expansion of human knowledge by the subculture of science, which puts a high value on the detection of error by testing, is a testimony to the high probability that this principle is not much in error.

In the case of human valuations it is a little harder to say what we mean by "error." Just as instability in images of fact under testing is strong evidence that these images were in error, so there are instabilities in structures of human valuations suggesting that image of value may be in error also. Where instability of valuation structures arises because they lead into the destruction of the culture that holds them, as may well have been the case with the followers of Moloch in Carthage and the followers of Hitler in Germany, the case for valuation error is very strong! Such instability may also arise because of the perception of "hypocrisy"—logical inconsistencies. The test of survival may not be an absolute test, but it is certainly an important one, and this suggests that the concept of pathological human valuation structures, which move societies toward situations that are eventually recognized as being worse rather than better, is by no means absurd. On this the hope for human betterment rests. The nineteenth-century belief in the inevitability of "progress" may have been naive and a special circumstance at the time. As in all evolutionary processes there are catastrophes and ups and downs, but the evidence for directionality in the evolutionary process is overwhelming, especially toward complexity, and human knowledge certainly participates in this evolutionary process. It has a strong tendency to increase, both in complexity and what might be called realism—that is, correspondence to some "real world." The same kind of evolutionary process also produces complexity in human valuation processes, and while there is pathological as well as desirable complexity, this complexity is not equivalent to the ultimate "goodness" as we have used the term, as it is only one of the virtues. Nevertheless there is evidence that we do, over the long haul, learn how to learn, and this includes learning how to evaluate and finding that something like progress in human valuations is a viable concept and a reasonable hope.

The greatest cause for pessimism at the moment is the apparent stability of the set of valuations that leads into violence, national defense, and the eventual destruction of the human race in historic time by nuclear war. The destruction of the human race by the present system of valuation would certainly indicate that it does not have much survival value, but that reflection is not particularly cheering. It is precisely the observation, however, of the evolutionary process in human valuations and the fact that these valuations do change—and often away from the pathological modes that do not lead to survival—that indicates that there is at least a reasonable hope that human evaluations will change toward a survival pattern and that this will happen in the world as a total system.

REFERENCES

BARNARD, C. I. (1938) The Functions of the Executive. Cambridge, MA: Harvard University Press.

BENOIT, E. (1980) Progress and Survival: An Essay on the Future of Mankind. New York: Praeger.

BOULDING, K. E. (1981) Ecodynamics. Beverly Hills, CA: Sage.

———and T. MUKERJEE [eds.] (1972) Economic Imperialism: A Book of Readings. Ann Arbor: University of Michigan Press.

BROWN, L. (1984) The State of the World. A Worldwatch Institute Report on Progress Towards a Sustainable Society. New York: W. W. Norton.

CRICK, F. (1981) Life Itself: Its Origin and Nature. New York: Simon & Schuster.

de CHARDIN, P. T. (1959) The Phenomenon of Man. New York: Harper & Row.

LOVELOCK, J. E. (1979) Gaia: A New Look at Life on Earth. New York: Oxford University Press.

MEADOWS, D. H. et al. (1972) The Limits to Growth. Report from the Club of Rome's Project on the Predicament of Mankind. New York: Universe Books.

MILGRAM, S. (1974) Obedience to Authority: An Experimental View. New York: Harper & Row.

National Research Council Climate Board (1983) Carbon Dioxide: Assessment of a Changing Climate. Washington, DC: National Academy Press.

National Research Council Committee on Nuclear and Alternative Energy Systems [CONAES] (1980) Energy in Transition 1985-2010: Final Report of the Committee on Nuclear and Alternative Energy Systems. San Francisco: W. H. Freeman.

PRIBRAM, K. H. (1983) "The brain, cognitive commodities, and the enfolded order," in K. E. Boulding and L. Senesh (eds.) The Optimum Utilization of Knowledge. Boulder, CO: Westview Press.

PRINGLE, J. W. S. (1956) "On the parallel between learning and evolution." General Systems Yearbook 1: 90-110.

SAGAN, C. (1983) "Nuclear war and climatic catastrophe." Foreign Affairs 62, 2: 257-292.

SCHELL, J. (1982) The Fate of the Earth. New York: Knopf.

SCHELLING, T. C. (1960) The Strategy of Conflict. Cambridge, MA: Harvard University Press.

SHANNON, C. E. and W. WEAVER (1964) The Mathematical Theory of Communication. Urbana: University of Illinois Press.

SIMON, J. L. (1981) The Ultimate Resource. Princeton, NJ: Princeton University Press.

SMITH, A. (1937) The Wealth of Nations. New York: Modern Library.

STOUFFER, S. A. et al. (1950) The American Soldier: Studies in Social Psychology in World War II. Princeton, NJ: Princeton University Press.

THOMPSON, W. D. (1962) On Growth and Form (2nd ed.). New York: Cambridge University Press.

TIGER, L. and R. FOX (1972) The Imperial Animal. New York: Dell.

WADDINGTON, C. H. (1962) The Nature of Life. New York: Atheneum.

WHORF, B. (1969) Language, Thought, and Reality. Cambridge, MA: Technology Press.

WIENER, N. (1948) Cybernetics. New York: John Wiley.

INDEX

ABOUT THE AUTHOR

KENNETH E. BOULDING is one of the magisterial figures in the field of social science. He has served as president of six major scholarly societies (American Association for the Advancement of Science, American Economic Association, International Studies Association, Peace Research Society, Society for General Systems Research, and Association for the Study of Grants Economy). He has taught at universities in seven countries, authored over thirty books and hundreds of articles, pamphlets, and chapters on numerous topics (including a book of poetry), and is the recipient of thirty-one honorary degrees and a variety of other awards. He and his wife, Elise, are among the founders of the field of peace and conflict research. Boulding is currently Distinguished Professor of Economics Emeritus at the University of Colorado and a Research Associate and Project Director of the Program of Research on Political and Economic Change in the university's Institute of Behavioral Science.